PRENTICE-HALL *GREEK DRAMA SERIES*

Series Editors

ERIC A. HAVELOCK, *Sterling Professor of Classics, Yale University*
MAYNARD MACK, *Sterling Professor of English, Yale University*

AESCHYLUS

Translated with commentary by

Agamemnon	Hugh Lloyd-Jones
The Eumenides	Hugh Lloyd-Jones
The Libation Bearers	Hugh Lloyd-Jones
The Persians	Anthony J. Podlecki
Prometheus Bound	Eric A. Havelock
The Seven Against Thebes	Christopher M. Dawson

SOPHOCLES

Ajax	Adam M. Parry
Antigone	Anne Amory
Electra	William Sale
Oedipus at Colonus	Joseph A. Russo
Oedipus the King	Thomas Gould
Philoctetes	William Arrowsmith
The Women of Trachis	Peter W. Rose

EURIPIDES

Alcestis	Charles Rowan Beye
The Bacchae	Geoffrey S. Kirk
Electra	Wesley Smith
Heracles	Christian Wolff
Hippolytus	Gilbert & Sally Lawall
Ion	Anne Pippin Burnett
Iphigeneia at Aulis	Kenneth Cavander
Medea	Bernard M. W. Knox
The Suppliants	A. Thomas Cole

The remaining nine plays are in preparation.

THE LIBATION BEARERS

BY ÆSCHYLUS

A Translation with Commentary by
HUGH LLOYD-JONES
Regius Professor of Greek
Oxford University

with a series introduction by Eric A. Havelock

PRENTICE-HALL, INC., ENGLEWOOD CLIFFS, N.J.

C13–535385–8
P13–535377–7

Library of Congress Catalog Card Number: 70–102283
Printed in the United States of America

Current Printing (last number):
10 9 8 7 6 5 4 3 2 1

PRENTICE-HALL INTERNATIONAL, INC. *London*
PRENTICE-HALL OF AUSTRALIA, PTY. LTD. *Sydney*
PRENTICE-HALL OF CANADA, LTD. *Toronto*
PRENTICE-HALL OF INDIA PRIVATE LIMITED *New Delhi*
PRENTICE-HALL OF JAPAN, INC. *Tokyo*

CONTENTS

FOREWORD TO THE SERIES

The Prentice-Hall Greek Drama Series will contain when completed the surviving tragedies of the Athenian stage. It offers each play in a separate inexpensive volume, so that readers may make their own personal selection rather than have the choice made for them, as is commonly the result when translations are issued in collective groups. It also offers each play in a context of exacting scholarship which seeks to make available to Greekless readers what the original Greek audiences responded to as they watched and listened to a performance. Under the English dress, in short, as far as humanly possible the Greek identity has been accentuated rather than obscured. Supported here by extensive introductions, notes, and appendices (in each case the work of an authority who has given painstaking attention to the full meanings of the text) and printed in a manner to exhibit their great varieties of formal structure, they step forth, untrammeled by preconceptions and conventional categorizations, as the highly individual creations they were when first performed.

The notes printed at the foot of each page to accompany the appropriate lines are in the first instance conceived as a corrective to shortcomings that no translation can avoid and should therefore be considered as in some sense an extension of the text. They testify to the fact that all translations in varying degree must indulge an element of deception, and they serve as a running attempt to explain its character and define its extent. In addition to this, they undertake to instruct the reader about conventions of idiom and imagery, of legend and allusion, which are native to the Greek situation and indispensable to a proper understanding of it. They aim also to get to the heart of the play as a work of art, exposing and explicating its often complex design in the hope that the reader thus aided will experience for himself its overwhelming dramatic effect.

M. M.

THE ATHENIAN DRAMATISTS

(Dates attested or probable are italicized)

AESCHYLUS	SOPHOCLES	EURIPIDES
525–456	*497/6–405/4*	*485/4–406/5*

Total production: c.90	Total production: c.125	Total production: c.92
Surviving plays: 7	Surviving plays: 7*	Surviving plays: 17*
First success *485*	First success *469*	First success *441*

AESCHYLUS	SOPHOCLES	EURIPIDES
The Persians 472		
The Seven Against Thebes 467		
The Suppliants 463?	*Ajax 460–45?* (date unknown—probably the earliest)	
Oresteia 458 (*Agamemnon, The Libation Bearers, The Eumenides*)	*Antigone 442–41*	*Alcestis 438*
Prometheus Bound (date unknown probably late)	*The Women of Trachis* (date unknown)	*Medea 431* *The Children of Heracles* c. 430–20
	Oedipus the King 429–25?	*Hippolytus 428* *Hecuba* c. 425 *The Suppliants* c. 420
	Electra 420–10	*Heracles* c. 420–16? *Andromache* c. 419 *Electra* c. *415–13* *The Trojan Women 415* *Helen 412* *Iphigeneia in Tauris* c. *412* *The Phoenician Women 410–9*
	Philoctetes 409	*Orestes 408* *Ion* c. *408?* *The Bacchae* c. *406* (produced posthumously)
	Oedipus at Colonus c. *406–5* (produced posthumously)	*Iphigeneia at Aulis 406* (produced posthumously)

* disregarding *The Ichneutae* of Sophocles and *The Cyclops* and *Rhesus* of Euripides which are not tragedies.

INTRODUCTION TO THE SERIES

1. GREEK TRAGEDY TODAY

The table of the three tragedians and their productions facing this page reveals a situation which, judged by our experience of European drama since the Greeks, is, to say the least, unusual. The total of thirty-one plays was composed within a span of about sixty-five years, between 472 and 406 B.C., and that ends the story. It is as though the history of the English drama were confined to the Elizabethans and the Jacobeans and then closed. These thirty-one are survivors—a mere handful—of an originally enormous total. The three playwrights between them are credited with over three hundred titles, and the plays of their competitors, which except for isolated fragments and notices have now vanished from the record, are uncountable.

These facts shed light upon a familiar paradox: Classic Greek drama is at once parochial and universal, narrowly concentrated upon recurrent motifs, characters, and situations, yet always able to evoke a response at a level which is fundamental and general. Most of these hundreds of plays were composed in the years between the defeat of the Persians by the Greeks at Salamis in 480 B.C. and the defeat of Athens by Sparta in 404 B.C.; they were produced for audiences in Athens and in Attica, that small canton district which contains the city and is itself circumscribed by the sea and the mountains. The limits of history and geography surrounding them are therefore narrow and intense. Greek tragedy is Attic and Athenian not accidentally but essentially, and this fact cannot but have had strong influence in the dramatic choices made by the playwrights as they selected situation, theme, and characters. The vast bulk of the lost productions, had it been preserved, would, one suspects, retain interest today mainly for specialists and antiquarians. There is indeed a good deal of antiquarianism in the plays we do have. But they are products of their authors' maturity, none composed at an age earlier than forty-five. Their preservation, if we except a few plays of Euripides, reflects some value judgments passed in antiquity; they were on the whole better able to withstand changes of taste and fashion and shifts in the character and nationality of audiences and critics.

The present age has come to recognize a new-found affinity with them. During the last century and the early part of the present one, when study of the classics was still dominant in education, Greek drama was read and esteemed as an exercise in the grand style, a mirror of the eternal verities and familiar moral imperatives. Even Euripides, the least tractable of the three from the moral standpoint, was credited with a desire to set the world right. By and large, the watchword the Victorians heard in the plays was not danger but decorum. Today, a generation which has known frustration and disillusionment—desperately demanding some private identity within a society which seems imprisoned and perhaps doomed by its own prior commitments—can view these plays with clearer eyes for what they are: portrayals of the human dilemma, which forswear the luxury of moral confidence and assured solutions. Here are sufferings disproportionate to the original error, characters caught and trapped in situations which are too much for them and for which they are only partly responsible. Here are pity and terror treated as facts of life with which one must come to terms. Here finally is defiance combined with a fatalism which accepts the tragic scene even at the moment of its repudiation. The watchword we listen to today is not decorum but danger. For the children of men who now inherit the earth it is therefore possible to respond to the classic tragedy of the Greeks with a directness denied to the more secure temper of their forebears.

Translators of Greek drama face a difficult choice between editing the Greek into language which will appeal to the modern sensibility, or offering a version which attempts as close an approximation as possible to the form and content of the original. The present series has been conceived on the assumption that since form and content hang together, the one cannot be paraphrased without damaging the other. The damage usually is done by suppressing those features of the original which affront the modern sensibility, while exaggerating those that do not. Quite commonly the operatic form of the plays is in a modern version played down or even ignored, and the temptation is always strong so to interpret the plots as to center interest upon characters at the expense of situation. The versions offered in this series, while modest in their pretensions, have sought to maintain fidelity to that original convention of the Greek which divided the diction of a play between choric and lyric portions on the one hand and spoken dialogue on the other. The two together constituted the total dramatic statement, which was thus partly sung and partly recited, and they are here printed in different typefaces to bring out more clearly the way in which the play's structure is articulated. Passages in hexameters, anapests, and trochaic tetrameters were either sung or chanted, and accordingly are printed here as lyric. The notes also make some attempt to indicate the metrical arrangements practiced in the lyric portions and the emotional effects produced. To transfer these effects in translation from an inflected tongue quantitatively scanned is impossible, and the aids offered are therefore directed to the imagination of the reader rather than to his ear.

2. THE DRAMATISTS

The alienation of the artist is not a condition which the Greeks of the classical age would readily have understood. The three Greek tragedians were Attic born and men of their time, participating, as the record indicates, in the political and social life of their community. Their plays accordingly expose, examine, and question the values of Greek society, but they do not reformulate and they do not reject. This being said, one must add that differences of style and approach between them are marked. The grandiloquence of Aeschylus becomes an appropriate instrument for expressing the confident ethos of the Athenian democracy and a theology which would justify the ways of Zeus to men. In the more stringent style of Sophocles, the tragic hero and heroine endure an exposure which is often ironic but which penetrates to the core of their dilemma, while their essential dignity is preserved and even enhanced. Euripides, the "most tragic" of the three, comes nearest to stepping outside his society. His later plays in particular tend to place the traditional norms of heroic and aristocratic leadership in an equivocal light. But his plots, as they enlarge the roles of women, children, servants, and slaves, remain faithful also to the changing mores and manners which increasingly foreshadowed the individualism of the Hellenistic age.

AESCHYLUS was born c. 525–24 at Eleusis near Athens of an aristocratic family (*eupatrid*). At thirty-five he fought at Marathon, where his brother fell gloriously; he may have also fought at Salamis.

He paid two visits to the court of Hieron in Sicily, who was the patron likewise of Pindar, Bacchylides, and Simonides. At the first visit he composed a play for the court celebrating Hieron's founding of the new city of Aetna (after 476); the second visit was terminated by his death at Gela in his seventieth year (456), where an epitaph on his monument celebrated his service at Marathon. An Athenian decree subsequently provided for the revival of any of his plays at public expense. Though he was preceded in the composition of tragic drama by the semi-legendary Thespis, Aeschylus is for practical purposes the "founder" of this unique art form, combining choric performance with a plot supported by dialogue between two, later three, actors. He was both composer and actor-manager, taking leads himself in some of his plays, probably the early ones. He is credited with developing the conventions of grandiloquent diction, rich costuming, formal dance figures, and some degree of spectacular effect. Although he died only about fifty years before *The Frogs* appeared, by Aristophanes' day his life was already a legend. Later stories about him (e.g., that he was an "initiate" who betrayed the secret of the Mysteries, or that he retired to Sicily in discomfiture for a variety of alleged reasons) are probably the inventions of an age more biographically inclined than his own.

SOPHOCLES was born c. 496 of an affluent family at Colonus near Athens. Known for his good looks, he was also an accomplished dancer and lyre player who, at age sixteen, was selected to lead the paean of victory after Salamis. He was taught by Lamprus, a famous master of the traditional music. He played roles in some of his own early productions, but later desisted, because of his weak voice. He took considerable part in public life. In 443–42 he was imperial treasurer; he was elected general twice—once in 440, the year in which Pericles suppressed the revolt of Samos, and again at a later date as colleague of Nicias; also, in 413, when he was over eighty years old, he was appointed one of the special commissioners (*probouloi*) to review the aftermath of the Sicilian disaster. He held a lay priesthood in the cult of a local deity of healing and allowed his own house to serve as a shrine of Asclepius pending the completion of a temple. He founded an Association (*thiasos*) of the Muses (something like a literary club). Polygnotus painted a portrait of him holding the lyre, which was hung in the picture gallery on the Acropolis. Tradition connects him with prominent men of letters, such as Ion of Chios, Herodotus (there are discernible points of contact between the History and the plays), and Archelaus the philosopher. In 406 he mourned the death of his younger contemporary Euripides in a public appearance with actors and chorus at the rehearsal (*proagon*) for the Great Dionysia. Some months later he died, at the age of ninety. He was remembered and celebrated as an example of the fortunate life, genial, accomplished, and serene.

EURIPIDES was born c. 485 at Phlya in Attica, probably of a good family. He made his home in Salamis, probably on an estate of his father, where it is said he composed in a cave by the sea. He held a lay priesthood in the cult of Zeus at his birthplace. Tradition, supported by hints in Old Comedy and the internal evidence of his own plays, connects him with the leading sophistic and philosophical circles of the day: Anaxagoras, Archelaus, Prodicus, Protagoras, and above all Socrates, said to be an admirer of his plays. In musical composition, he was assisted by a certain Cephisophon; this collaboration was probably a common practice. He served on an embassy to Syracuse (date unknown) and composed a public elegy in 413 for the Athenian soldiers fallen in Sicily. Prisoners in the quarries are said to have won release from their captors by reciting his choruses. He appears to have preferred a life of some seclusion, surrounded by his household. In 408–7 he left Athens for the north. He stayed initially at Magnesia in Thessaly, where he was received with honors, and then at the court of Archelaus of Macedon. There, in addition to a court play composed in the king's honor, he produced *The Bacchae*, his last extant work. He died there in 406. Buried in Macedonia he was memorialized by a cenotaph at Athens. Some of his plays were produced posthumously by one of his three sons. A good deal of the tradition surrounding his parentage, domestic life, personal character, and contemporary reputation in Athens is unfriendly to him; but it is also unreliable, depending as it probably does on the satirical treatment which he often received from the comic poets.

3. THE TIMES

In 525, when Aeschylus was born, the "tyranny" established at Athens under Pisistratus and his sons was still in power. When he was five years old, the tyrants were expelled, and a series of constitutional changes began which were to result in the establishment of complete democracy.

Abroad, the Persian Empire, founded by Cyrus the Great, had already absorbed all of Asia Minor and extended its sway over the Ionian Greeks. The year of Aeschylus' birth had been marked by the Persian conquest of Egypt, followed by that of Babylon. When he was sixteen, the Ionian Greeks revolted against their Persian masters, were defeated and partially enslaved (494), after which the Persian power sought to extend its conquests to the Greek mainland. This attempt, repulsed at Marathon (490), was finally defeated at Salamis, Plataea, and Mycale (480–79). The Greeks in turn, under the leadership of Athens, liberated the Ionians from Persian control and established the Confederacy of Delos to preserve the liberty thus gained.

By degrees, this alliance was transformed into the Athenian Empire, governed by an ascendant and confident democracy, under the leadership of many eminent men, none more so than Pericles, whose political power lasted from about 460 to his death in 429. The empire, though supported as a defense against Persia, became the natural target of disaffected allies, who found themselves becoming subjects, and of the jealousy of other Greek states, notably Sparta and Corinth. In 432 a Peloponnesian coalition under Spartan leadership opened hostilities with Athens, ostensibly to free Greece from her yoke. The war lasted, with an interval of armistice, till 404, when Athens, exhausted and over-extended by commitments, lost her last naval protection and was besieged and captured by the Peloponnesian forces.

Within the two years preceding this event, Euripides and Sophocles had both died. The works of the three dramatists were therefore composed during an expansive age in which democracy at home was matched by imperialism abroad. The repulse of the foreign invader was followed by the extension of Athenian commerce and influence throughout the eastern Mediterranean, and to some extent in the west also. This brought in the revenues and also encouraged the confidence in leadership which supported Pericles' ambitious policies and adorned the Acropolis with those public buildings, unmatched in purity of style, which still stand there.

But before the last plays were written, the strain of an exhausting and demoralizing war with fellow Greeks was beginning to tell, and in a moment of crisis even the democratic constitution had been called in question (411). For Aeschylus, his city's history had been an unbroken success story. In the lifetime of his two successors, she confronted an increasing series of problems, military, political, and social, which proved too much even for her energies to sustain.

4. GREEK THEATRICAL PERFORMANCE

The twelfth chapter of Aristotle's *Poetics* contains the following statement:

> . . . The quantitative sections . . . into which a tragedy is divided are the following: *prologos, epeisodion, exodos,* and the choral part, itself subdivided into *parodos* and *stasima.* These occur in all tragedies; there may also be actors' songs and *kommoi.*

The *prologos* is that whole section which precedes the entrance of the chorus; the *epeisodion* is a whole section between complete choral odes; the *exodos* is that whole section of a tragedy which is not followed by a choral ode. In the choral part, the entrance song (*parodos*) is the first complete statement of the chorus, a *stasimon* is a song of the chorus without anapests or trochees; a *kommos* is a dirge in which actors and chorus join. . . .*

Students in English literature and other fields are likely to have been introduced to this famous passage. Yet scarcely any statement about Greek drama has caused more misunderstanding. It is schematic when it should be tentative, and definitive when it should be approximate. It has encouraged the presumption, widely held, that Greek plays were constructed according to a standard model from which, to be sure, the dramatist might diverge on occasion, but which nevertheless was his model: A prologue was followed by a choric entrance, for which anapests were supposedly the normal vehicle, and this by dialogue divided into episodes separated by full choruses, and concluded by an exit after the last chorus. No doubt the anonymous author (Aristotle could scarcely have been so dogmatic or so wrong) reflects those standards of mechanical formalism current in the period of the drama's decline. The key statement, "These occur in all tragedies," is false. The suggestion that actors' songs and *kommoi* (duets, trios, and quartets) were additions to the standard form is equally false. In Aeschylus alone, the reader will discover that neither his *The Persians* nor his *The Suppliants* has either *prologos* or *exodos* (applying these terms as defined in the *Poetics*). If the *Prometheus Bound* has a *parodos*, it is technically a *kommos*, that is, a duet shared between Prometheus and the chorus. Two of the *stasima*, or choric odes, in *The Eumenides* are interrupted by nonchoric iambics. It would be interesting to know how the author of these remarks would apply his definition of *exodos* to *Agamemnon*. On his terms, the *exodos* extends from lines 1035 to 1673, but it includes one elaborate lyric duet sung by Cassandra and chorus, then the murder of Agamemnon, then an equally elaborate duet sung by Clytemnestra and chorus. The *parodos* of *The Seven Against Thebes* is not in anapests, nor is that of *The Eumenides*, and the *exodos* of *The Eumenides* is, in effect, an elaborate lyric trio shared between Athena and two different choruses.

---

* Translation by G. M. A. Grube, from *Aristotle on Poetry and Style.* New York: Liberal Arts Press, 1958.

No doubt the practice of Sophocles encouraged schematization, but even his practice often included in the *exodos* the climactic portions of the drama. *Oedipus the King* is an example. The practice of Euripides often reverts to the fluidity characteristics of Aeschylus. The fact seems to be that the whole conception of a tragedy as consisting of quantitative parts is erroneous, and the reader is best advised to approach each play as, in some sense, a new creation. Hence, though translators in this series may from time to time use the classic, or neoclassic, terms of the *Poetics*, they may equally be forced to apply modern terminology and speak of choric or lyric songs, of acts and scenes, of entrances, exits, and finales, according as the specific structure of any given play may require.

The conditions of production have never since been duplicated, and since they affect the way the plays were written, a word about them is in order. Performances took place in the open air. The audience sat on benches inserted into the slope of a recessed hillside. Chorus and actors shared not a stage but a circular dancing floor, on which the audience looked down. Thus, the Greek play remained a spectacle for the eye, as well as a verbal and musical delight to the ear, particularly as the figures executed in the dances produced patterns which an elevated angle of vision could appreciate. The audience was rarely asked to imagine the action as taking place in a closed room. Forecourts and courtyards and the street itself predominate as settings under the Mediterranean sky, and that sky itself, as the reader will discover, is never very far away from the characters' thought and speech.

At the back of the dancing floor stood a temporary wooden structure, the proscenium, with a central and two side doors and a flat roof. The doors were used for entrances and exits, the roof as a platform for appearances that called for an elevated position (those of gods, and sometimes human beings like the Watchman in the opening scene of *Agamemnon*). Behind the proscenium the actors could change their costumes, which were formalized to indicate sex, age, and social status. It is important to distinguish the *characters* who appear in a given play from the *actors* who played their parts. The former, while few by Shakespearean standards, considerably outnumbered the latter, who were rationed to two in some plays, three in most (four occasionally and doubtfully). The practical effect was that not more than two or three speaking parts could be carried on at any one time, so that at least some of the characters had to be played by different actors at different times, and the actors, relying on costume changes, had to be prepared to change their roles with rapidity. This ancient convention had an important result: The personality of the actor was severed from the role he played—this was also an effect of his mask—and reduced in importance (that is, until conventions changed in the Hellenistic age); and hence the burden of dramatic emphasis had to be carried entirely by the language, whoever happened to be speaking it. This is one reason why the verbal virtuosity of Greek tragedy has never been surpassed, even by Shakespeare.

The limitation of actors to two or three was undoubtedly related to a practical necessity. To examine (as one can do very easily in the typography employed in this series) the proportions of lyric to dialogue in a Greek play—that is, of sung to spoken parts, as these are assigned to individual actors (ignoring the chorus)—is to discover that the actors, and not just the chorus, had to have excellent singing voices enabling them to sustain solos, duets, trios and quartets. Even if they were assigned on a trial basis—the precise details of selection are disputable—the supply of suitable voices would be limited, and would require rationing among several plays competing simultaneously.

The standard phrase to describe authorship was "to teach a chorus," while "to grant a chorus" indicated the procedures of acceptance which put a play in production. Both seem to argue for the priority of the chorus in the classic Greek conception though the degree of priority is again a matter of dispute. The assembling and training of a group of singers and dancers (the total number is in dispute and may have varied) obviously took the most time, money, and skill. The expense was borne partly by the state and partly by private patrons, though the arrangements changed somewhat in the course of time. The playwright became his own producer, exercising a degree of control which is reflected in the tight unity of most Greek plays, exhibiting as they do something of the symmetry of Greek architecture.

The lyrics were accompanied by woodwinds, and the anapests, trochaic tetrameters, and dactyls were chanted, very possibly to the accompaniment of strings. The term chorus, however, indicates not singers but dancers, just as the terms strophe and antistrophe (which are Hellenistic), attached to symmetrical stanzas, originally indicated the turns and counter-turns of symmetrical dance patterns. This reminds us that, besides the music, we have lost the choreography, which was executed in figures of varying complexity. Conventions which today we would assign to ballet, opera, and oratorio are in Greek drama combined with a series of speaking parts to make something that we call by analogy a stage play, but which in fact is an ensemble uniquely Greek and classical and somewhat alien to modern expectations. It is a mistake, as any reader of *Agamemnon* or *Hippolytus* will discover, to think of plot as being restricted to the speaking parts. Lyric and dialogue are partners in the task of forwarding the action and exposing character and motive.

Though the place of performance of most but not all of these plays was the Theater of Dionysus on the southeast slope of the Acropolis and though one major occasion for the competition was the festival of the City Dionysia, this connection with the god and his cult—contrary to some widely held opinion—seems to have left no perceptible mark on the plays we have. *The Bacchae*, which might appear to be an exception, was not composed originally for performance in Athens, and its setting, we should note, is Theban. Even the Theater of Dionysus itself had replaced a more primitive arrangement in the market place. Furthermore tragic competitions were not restricted to the Dionysia. Latterly at least, they were also offered at the spring festival of the Lenaea. The link between Dionysus and the Greek theater became intimate in the Hellenistic age; their relationship in the sixth and fifth centuries is a matter of dispute, and was possibly somewhat fortuitous. Three prizes were awarded for first, second, and third places, and though special judges were selected for this purpose, they made their decision in front of the audience, which did not hesitate to register its own preferences. Thus the plays were composed for the Athenian public, not for an esoteric minority. Appeals to contemporary feeling on political and social issues are certainly not to be excluded on a priori grounds as violating the purity of Greek art. The reader himself will note without learned assistance how frequently a plot or episode manages to exploit Athenian pride and patriotism.

These original conditions of performance, as we have said, helped to mould the character of the text. The simplicity of the early playing area prompted the use of "verbal scenery" (instead of props and physical effects) and a "program" of plot and characters incorporated in the diction, most of it in the "prologue." But the plays were then revived continuously for centuries, during which time the details of staging, costumes, masks, the formal rules of dramaturgy, the profession of acting, and the construction of the theater itself, were all elaborated and formalized, even to some extent "modernized." The reader should be warned that in current handbooks on the subject he is likely to encounter much which draws on testimonies from these later periods, and which cannot be authenticated for the simpler but more creative conditions of the fifth century B.C.

E. A. H.

ON THE METRES OF GREEK TRAGEDY

One difference between Attic tragedy and opera is the domination of words over music. The music was there, in the choral passages, perhaps in all passages other than pure dialogue. But the rhythm of the words controlled the music. This is clearly to be inferred from the *strophic* structure of the full choral ode. A *strophe*, an elaborate series of metric elements arranged in a complex and unique pattern, will be followed by an *antistrophe* which repeats that pattern precisely, a long syllable in the one will match a long syllable in the other, and a short will match a short. This would be unthinkable as much in modern operatic forms as in medieval chant, where syllables can be lengthened or shortened, or can receive varying stress, as the rhythm of the music requires.

Greek metre depends on an alternation of long and short syllables, and not, as in English verse, on a sequence of stressed and unstressed syllables. In the main, there were three types of metre. First, in the dialogue, and in such passages as the spoken prologue and messengers' speeches, we have an iambic metre probably unaccompanied by music. It is called iambic trimeter because it can be best analyzed into three dipodies of two iambs each. There is a good analogy here with English blank verse, although the Greek line had six iambs rather than five as in English, and although the Greek line was stricter than the English analogue; in Greek comedy a good reader can instantly pick out a quoted or a parodied tragic trimeter from the surrounding comic trimeters by the greater regularity of the former. A typical line is 1. 12 of *Oedipus the King*:

ho pasi kleinos Oidipus kalumenos
the famous man whom all men know as Oedipus

where the single vertical represents the metrical division into dipodies, the double vertical the regular *caesura*, or word-ending within the third or fourth iambic foot.

When the chorus enter the orchestra in the *parodos*, again when they leave in the *exodos*, and in other passages, such as the introduction of new characters after a choral ode, the chorus, or one of the main characters, often speak in anapests. This metre can be arranged in lines, but in fact falls into *systems*, or long sequences, since there is no real metrical break at the end of the conventionally arranged lines. The series of anapests, that is, simply goes on until a shortened foot, a single syllable, coinciding with a verse-pause, ends the *system*. Thus we get ᵕᵕ_ ᵕᵕ_ . . . . . ᵕᵕ_ _. This is clearly a marching rhythm, and was usually accompanied by linear movement (on or off stage) by chorus or actors. Though some variations are allowed, spondees (_ _) or dactyls (_ᵕᵕ) sometimes replacing the anapests (e.g., ᵕᵕ_ | _ _ | ᵕᵕ_ | _ᵕᵕ | ᵕᵕ_, etc. is possible), the anapestic is the steadiest, most driving, metre in Greek drama. Musically, it was probably between dialogue and choral song, probably accompanied by a simple melody and chanted rather than spoken, in a manner somewhat like *recitative*.

The full choral ode is an elaborate metrical, musical, and choreographic structure. In a modern English text, these odes often look like what used to be called *free verse*. They are in fact extremely tight structures, as the correspondence between strophe and antistrophe reveals. They are like free verse only in that each ode is a metrically unique creation: The metres are made up of known elements, but these elements are arranged into a pattern peculiar to the single ode.

The metrical structure of choral odes requires a book for adequate description. But three common types of metrical elements in them can be noted here. First *iambic*: here we have usually varied and syncopated iambic forms, appearing as short metrical cola, or sections; for example,

ᵕ_ ᵕ_ | ʌ _ ᵕ _ | ᵕ_ ʌ _

ᵕ_ ᵕ_ | ʌ _ ᵕ _ | ᵕ_ ʌ _

where the caret shows the missing syllable which would have made each of the three parts of these two cola (appearing as *lines* in our text) a standard iambic dipody. This metre is crisp and lively and relatively uncomplicated. In origin, it is closer to speech than other choral metres: In the hands of Aeschylus, it could reach (as in the choral odes of *Agamemnon*) an unparalleled religious and dramatic solemnity.

ON THE METRES OF GREEK TRAGEDY

The favorite choral metre of Sophocles was the Aeolic (so-called because it appears in the lyric poetry of the Aeolic poets Sappho and Alcaeus) composed of elements which appear to be expanded choriambs (– ᴗ ᴗ –) with various combinations preceding and following them. The most common element is the glyconic – ᴗ – ᴗ ᴗ – ᴗ –; but endless variations are possible. It is perhaps the most mellifluous, and the most capable of subtle modulation of all choral metres. Sometimes iambic elements, and these sometimes in the form of a series of short syllables, will be introduced with great dramatic effect in Aeolic sequence; and sometimes the Aeolic metre will be turned to the rapid and epic movement of a dactylic sequence (– ᴗ ᴗ – ᴗ ᴗ . . .). Both these variations occur, for example, in the great first stasimon of *Antigone* (332 f.).

The wildest and most eccentric metre is the *dochmiac*, which seems to consist of staccato and abruptly syncopated iambic elements, typical forms being ᴗ – – ᴗ – and ᴗ ᴗ ᴗ ᴗ ᴗ –. This metre is used to mark statements of great fear or grief. The *parodos* of *The Seven Against Thebes*, where the Theban women imagine their city taken, is an extended passage in dochmiacs. Another example is *Hippolytus*, 811 f., where the chorus lament the suicide of Phaedra. Here as often in dochmiac, lines of iambic trimeter, as in spoken dialogue, are interspersed (813, 819–28, etc.). This may correspond to a break in the music and dancing, a further dramatic representation of extreme anxiety.

These choral or sung metres are most often uttered by the chorus, but sometimes by a single character, in a monody, or more often, in a lyric dialogue with the chorus. This latter is called a *kommos*, literally (*self*-) *striking* or *lamentation*, because that is the usual mode of such passages. By its nature, the kommos is often in dochmiac metre.

These are three of the principal metrical forms in choral song. Each has its distinct *ethos*, or emotional tone; and this distinct emotion was elaborated and enhanced by the dancing as well as the music, both these parts of the overwhelming choral performance being composed so as to correspond to the metrical pattern.

Sometimes more special metres are used in choruses for more special effect, and we shall mention only two: (1) The chorus at the beginning of *Agamemnon* as they move from their marching anapests into song begin with a dactylic hexameter – ᴗ ᴗ – ᴗ ᴗ – ᴗ ᴗ – ᴗ ᴗ – ᴗ ᴗ – –, the metre of Homeric epic: that is clearly a deliberate recalling of the Homeric situation; (2) much of the *parodos* of *The*

Bacchae (e.g., 64 ff.) is an Ionic metre ◡◡‒ ‒ ◡◡‒ ‒, etc. That is because this metre was used in ritual hymns to Dionysus.

Finally, we should note the trochaic tetrameter ‒◡‒◡ ‒◡‒◡ ‒◡‒◡ ‒◡‒. A rapid and slightly rollicking form, this was said to be the original dialogue metre of tragedy, and its relative frequency in the early plays of Aeschylus may bear this out. It is a dialogue metre, is more formal than iambic trimeter, and expresses more hurry and agitation: e.g., *The Persians* 155–75, 215–48, where we note that for the Queen's long speech in 176–214, the metre reverts to the more conversational iambic trimeter.

The preceding is only a bare sketch of the intricacies, as well as the expressive possibilities, of Greek tragic metre. For fuller accounts (which, however, require some knowledge of Greek) see:

Oxford Classical Dictionary, article of *metre, Greek,* London: Oxford University Press, 1949.

D. S. Raven, *Greek Metre, an Introduction,* New York: Humanities Press, Inc., 1962.

W. J. W. Koster, *Traité de métrique grecque,* 2nd. ed., Leiden: Brill, 1953.

ADAM PARRY

INTRODUCTION

This version of Orestes' return and revenge was not the only one extant in antiquity, and it is of some interest to compare Aeschylus' account with those that preceded it. In *The Odyssey*, Zeus sends his messenger Hermes to Aegisthus, when Aegisthus is plotting the murder of Agamemnon, to warn him that if he carries out his plan Orestes will one day avenge the murder. Nonetheless, Aegisthus kills Agamemnon, and in due course Orestes returns from exile and kills Aegisthus. What happens to Clytemnestra is not revealed; she dies at the same time, but we are not told that Orestes kills her. Orestes himself returns to Argos from exile in Athens. The first author to have him spend his exile at the court of Strophius, the king of Phocis, seems to have been Agias, author of the post-Homeric epic *Nostoi*, which describes the return of the chief Greek heroes from Troy. This was probably a work of the seventh or sixth century; by that time the Delphic oracle had already become important, and the change may have been dictated by the wish to make Delphi, which lay in Phocian territory, prominent in the story.

Orestes' revenge was described in the *Oresteia* of the famous sixth-century lyric poet Stesichorus of Himera in Sicily. Unfortunately we know few details of his work, but he seems to have introduced the figure of Orestes' nurse, who according to Pindar saved Orestes from death at the hands of his father's murderers, and who plays a notable part in Aeschylus' drama. Both Stesichorus and Pindar call the nurse by heroic names; Aeschylus calls her by a servile name, in harmony with his presentation of her character (see 732 with note). Stesichorus also mentions the dream that warned Clytemnestra of her approaching end:

> To her there seemed to come a snake, his crest stained with blood; and then appeared the king, the son of Pleisthenes.

In this story the snake clearly stands for Agamemnon, but in Aeschylus' version of the dream it symbolizes Orestes (526f). More important, Stesichorus was probably the first author to describe how Orestes, because of matricide, is pursued by the Erinyes, the terrible beings from the world below whose function was to punish those who murdered their own kin. In Stesichorus, as in Aeschylus, Orestes is sustained by the advice and help of Apollo, the god of the Delphic Oracle; Stesichorus told how Apollo gives Orestes a bow with which to defend himself against the Erinyes. In Aeschylus, Orestes does not have to defend himself with actual weapons, but Apollo helps him first by granting him purification and then by his advocacy at his trial.

In Aeschylus, the place of Orestes' exile must be Phocis because of its connection with the oracle. Orestes returns accompanied by Pylades, son of the king of Phocis, who according to the usual legend later marries Orestes' sister Electra. Pylades may well be regarded as the spokesman of Apollo's oracle, for his only speech in the play is an injunction not to disobey the oracle's command (see 900–901 with note). But the connection with Athens that appears in Homer is equally important to Aeschylus. In the last play of the trilogy, it is in Athens that Orestes seeks refuge from the pursuit of the Erinyes, and it is an Athenian court, presided over by Athene herself, that acquits him of the charge brought against him.

The stage is dominated by the mound that represents Agamemnon's grave; Orestes and Pylades appear before it, and Orestes calls upon the gods to help revenge his father's murder. They are interrupted by the arrival of Orestes' sister Electra, accompanied by the slave-women from the palace who form the Chorus. The figure of Electra, so important in Greek tragedy, does not appear in Homer, where Agamemnon's daughters are called Chrysothemis, Laodice, and Iphianassa. As far as we know, Electra is mentioned first by Xanthus of the Sicilian city of Locri; he was an obscure lyric poet belonging to the same school as the more celebrated Stesichorus. In the present play the women of the Chorus describe themselves as captives taken in war, and, indeed, slaves were commonly captives in the world of Greek epic.

Electra and the slave-women have come to the grave because Clytemnestra has given a most surprising order—they are to offer a libation at the grave of Agamemnon. What accounts for her sudden wish to placate the spirit of the husband she has long ago murdered and consigned to a dishonored grave? We learn from the Parodos, the first ode sung by the Chorus, that it is because of a dream, whose exact details we learn only later. The Chorus knows that her effort at appeasement is bound to prove futile. For although the murderers of Agamemnon are at present all-powerful, the law of Zeus—that the doer must suffer—demands that eventually they must pay the penalty for the blood they have shed.

The story of Orestes' return does not call for the same frequent glimpses into past and future as the preceding story of the deaths of Agamemnon and Cassandra. The past is often mentioned, but its details are now familiar to the audience; the future—the pursuit of Orestes by the Erinyes and his eventual escape—the poet is concerned to keep uncertain. The first half of the play concentrates on Electra's recognition of Orestes and on the preparations for the attack on the usurpers. An all-important preliminary to these preparations is the great conjuration designed to arouse the ghost of Agamemnon and to ensure its active collaboration in the destruction of the murderers. The second part of the play shows how Orestes enters the palace and carries out his task. Only during the last act do the audience suddenly become aware that the Erinyes, who as they know would have pursued Orestes had he neglected to avenge his father, will now pursue him for the murder of his mother.

The sex and station of the Chorus render it especially suited to utter the bitter lamentations for Agamemnon's fate and for the tyranny of the usurpers in the first half of the play. Likewise, in the second half the Chorus is well suited to utter the passionate prayers for the victory and for the preservation of Orestes. But like the Chorus of *Agamemnon*, it is aware throughout that in the end Zeus and Justice are bound to triumph, and this knowledge relieves even the deep melancholy of the Parodos (22f). The Chorus remembers that blood once shed cannot be recalled, and touches on a motive that recurs again and again in the course of the trilogy, that blood once shed necessitates revenge. The Chorus is a party to Electra's decision to turn against her mother the power that Clytemnestra's offerings were supposed to exert. Terrified by the warning dream, Clytemnestra had sent them to the tomb to appease her husband's ghost. Throughout the great lyric scene in which brother and sister in alternation conjure their father's spirit to rise and strike against his murderers, the Chorus spurs them on with declarations of passionate hatred against the enemy and with reminders that Zeus will never allow such crimes to go unpunished. Afterward, the Chorus, together with Electra, listens to Orestes' instructions to those who wish to help him; then in the First Stasimon (585f) it dwells on the enormity of Clytemnestra's crimes, comparing her, after the fashion of tragic choruses, with the most monstrous criminals of the past and declaring that Justice and the Erinyes must soon take their revenge on her. After Orestes has made his entry into the palace and deceived his mother with the false report of his own death, the Chorus gives him material help by telling the Nurse to ask Aegisthus to come, not with his bodyguard, as Clytemnestra has instructed her, but alone. As the decisive moment approaches, the Chorus seconds Orestes and Pylades with a prayer to the gods whose assistance they most need, followed by an injunction to Orestes to fulfill Apollo's order with utter ruthlessness (the Second Stasimon, 783f). After the double killing, the Chorus sings a great hymn of triumph to Justice and Apollo, who have brought salvation to the house of Atreus. Nowhere does it doubt the rightness of Orestes' decision to kill his mother; nowhere does it apprehend that at the very moment of his triumph, he will be menaced by the same dangers that would have overwhelmed him had he refused to obey Apollo's oracle.

4

Aeschylus has no interest in character for its own sake, and this fact is especially easy to perceive here. Electra, who in Sophocles and Euripides will be a dominating figure, has the conventional qualities of a princess in the heroic age. Deeply loyal to her father and brother, bitterly hostile to her father's murderers, she is not yet required to exhibit the ferocious hatred portrayed in later tragedy. Scenes in which long-separated relatives became aware of one another's identity were to become part of the regular stock-in-trade of tragedy and, later, of the New Comedy of Menander and his contemporaries; the recognition of Orestes by Electra in this play is a simple and almost primitive, but also dignified and moving, example of the type. Euripides in his *Electra* derided both Electra's recognition of a lock of hair left by Orestes on his father's tomb and, still more, her recognition of her brother's footprints. Sharing his attitude, some modern critics have declared the footprints to be an interpolation, and they are careful to delete the passage in which Euripides made fun of them as being an interpolation made to ridicule a second interpolation in that of Aeschylus. Advocates of this theory fail to recognize that the technique of tragedy in Aeschylus' time was of a simplicity utterly removed from modern naturalism. When Electra voices her love for her restored brother, she echoes the famous words in which the Homeric Andromache voices her love for her husband Hector; the archaic beauty and simplicity of the recognition scene in *The Libation Bearers* is similar in feeling to the poetry of Homer.

Critics who have labored to read into Aeschylus' characters the individualism of Elizabethan or even of Ibsenian drama have had a hard time with the central figure of the last two plays of the *Oresteia*—the character from whom the trilogy takes its name. Orestes often speaks poetry of great richness, not to mention the lyrics that he sings during the great scene of conjuration; but of individuality he shows little trace. Near the beginning of the play (269f), he describes with horrifying vividness the awful fate that Apollo has warned him he will suffer if he neglects his duty to avenge his father, and he takes it as a matter of course that he can do nothing but obey. Even if he did not trust Apollo, he continues, he must win back his father's property, and he must not allow the

Argive people to remain subject to the tyranny of the usurpers. Modern critics whose minds have been dominated by the unconscious presuppositions dictated by modern drama have tried hard to show that Orestes can kill his mother only if he is spurred by the stimulus afforded by the conjuration scene. Their attempt is not successful (see note on Conjuration Scene, 306). The poet's words make it unambiguously clear that the purpose of the conjuration is to secure the all-important assistance of Agamemnon's ghost; nowhere is there the slightest evidence that Orestes has even considered the possibility of disobeying Apollo. After the conjuration, Orestes, speaking like a commander, tells his sympathizers of the parts required of them by a well-contrived strategic plan, which he goes on to carry out.

An unfortunate result of the eagerness of modern commentators to lay stress on Aeschylus as a thinker and religious poet has been their frequent neglect to observe that *The Libation Bearers,* like *Agamemnon,* is full of suspense, action, and skillfully contrived surprise. When Orestes comes to the supreme moment of confrontation with his mother, he meets each of her pleas with what is, from Apollo's point of view, the proper answer. Despite the stilted form of dialogue in which each actor speaks one line in turn, the scene not only brings out the poignancy of the tragic dilemma, but conveys the feelings of both participants. Only at the end does Orestes hesitate, and then only for a moment; then Pylades, the neighbor of Apollo, reminds him of his duty, and he obeys. Some of the critics who have found signs of hesitation in the earlier behavior of Orestes suppose the poet to have prepared the way for the madness that comes upon him during the final scene, when the Erinyes, visible only to his eye, come to pursue him. In fact no such signs can be discerned; in his conscious mind, at least, Aeschylus conceived the madness instilled by the Erinyes as a purely external visitation.

Aegisthus makes only a brief appearance in this play; more noteworthy is the appearance of Clytemnestra. The sinister ambiguity of her opening words of welcome (668f) shows that she is still the Clytemnestra of *Agamemnon.* Must the grief she expresses when she first hears the false report of her son's death be considered totally insincere (691f)? Perhaps not; but she acknowledges that she can only feel secure if the threat of her son's return is removed. The point is driven home when she assures the messenger that he will not be cheated of the reward commonly paid to the bearers of good news. Unmixed grief is shown only by Orestes' old Nurse, a humble figure who makes a brief but astonishingly vivid appearance that contrasts sharply with the stiff archaic dignity of the heroic characters. In the sculpture scenes depicting the battle of the Lapiths with the Centaurs on the west pediment of Zeus's temple at Olympia, the canons of prevailing taste did not permit the features of the heroes and heroic maidens or of the central figure of Apollo to express emotion; this was reserved for the ferocious and subhuman Centaurs. By a somewhat similar convention Aeschylus allows the Nurse a vivacious garrulity and a readiness to mention humble objects and pursuits that set her off from all other tragic characters, except the Guard in Sophocles' *Antigone*.

In its concluding words the Chorus, terrified by the sudden madness of Orestes, expresses the deepest uncertainty about the future. First came the Thyestean feast, then the death of Agamemnon. Is the house of Atreus now saved, or is it lost? At what point in time, they ask, will the might of destruction finally be lulled to sleep?

CHARACTERS

AEGISTHUS, *king of Argos*

CHORUS, *slave-women*

CLYTEMNESTRA, *queen of Argos*

ELECTRA, *daughter of* CLYTEMNESTRA

NURSE

ORESTES, *son of* CLYTEMNESTRA

PYLADES, *friend of* ORESTES

SLAVE

THE LIBATION BEARERS

Scene: the grave of AGAMEMNON. Enter ORESTES
and PYLADES.

MOOD - MOTIF - YOU WHO ARE UNDERGROUND.

ORESTES   Hermes of the earth, you who watch over your
   father's kingdom, *THE DEAD KILLING THE LIVING.*
be my preserver and fight beside me in answer to my prayer.
For I have come to this land, returning from my exile
   . . . . . .
And on the mound of this grave I cry to my father
to give ear, to listen . . .   5

Listen here you chthonics. . . .

Orestes: pronounce Ŏr·est'·ēs; Pylades: pronounce Pie'·lă·
dēs.

1   At the beginning of the play, perhaps as many as thirty
     lines are missing from the single manuscript. The first nine
     lines printed in the text were preserved through quotations
     by other authors. The meaning of the opening line is
     disputed between Euripides and Aeschylus in Aristophanes'
     The Frogs (1119f). Euripides thinks it means, "Hermes of
     the earth, who looked upon my father's murder"; Aeschylus
     thinks it means, "Hermes of the earth, who watches over
     your father's [i.e., Zeus's] kingdom." Some modern scholars
     say that Agamemnon is the father referred to, but there is

9

. . . a lock for Inachus in payment for my nurture,
and this second lock in token of my mourning.

* * * * * *

For I was not here to bewail your death, father,
nor did I stretch out my hand as your corpse was borne to
burial.

* * * * * *

Enter ELECTRA with the CHORUS of slave-women,
carrying libations to offer at the tomb.

What do I see? What is this company   10
of women coming in black robes
that meets my eye? To what event can I refer it?
Does some new disaster come upon the house?

---

little doubt that the interpretation of the Aristophanic
Aeschylus is right. It is relevant that Aeschylus sometimes
speaks of Hades, god of the underworld, as "the Zeus of
the dead" (see *Agam.* 1387 with my note). Hermes in his
aspect of Chthonios, "of the earth," was the intermediary
between the world of the dead and the world of the living.
He is therefore the most suitable god for ORESTES to invoke,
for he will soon have to establish communication with his
father's spirit to obtain help against his murderers.

6– *Inachus:* pronounce *Eye′·nă·khus:*

7   The Inachus was the principal river of Argos. It was customary for young men to offer a lock of hair to their country's rivers in return for the nurture the rivers were supposed
to provide. It was also customary to offer a lock to the dead.
Thus Achilles in *The Iliad* (23, 142) dedicates a lock on
Patroclus' tomb that the dead warrior would have given to
the river near his home in Thessaly, the Spercheius, had it
been his fate to survive the war and to return.

8   To take part in the obsequies of one's close kin, especially
parents, was a sacred duty not to be neglected except for
the gravest reasons.

Or shall I be right if I guess that they are bringing libations
to my father, meant to appease those below the earth?   15
It can be nothing else; yes, I seem to see advance
Electra, my sister, whose bitter grief
marks her out. O Zeus, grant that I may avenge the death
of my father, and of your grace fight on my side!
Pylades, let us stand out of the way, so that I may learn   20
for certain what this supplication of the women may import.

Enter ELECTRA *and the* CHORUS *of slave-women.*

STROPHE 1

CHORUS *Sent from the palace have I come*
to convey libations; my hands strike me sharp blows;
Crimson shows my cheek as I tear it,
with the furrow fresh-cut by my nails.   25
All my life long are lamentations my heart's food.
Ruining the linen texture,

---

14 Libations to the dead consisted of three offerings in a
defined order—first honey and milk, then wine, and finally
water. Normally, they would have been offered regularly at
the tomb ever since Agamemnon's death; in fact this was
the first such offering ever made there. Agamemnon had
been denied the proper rites of burial, a fact shocking to
Greek religious sentiment (see *Agam.* 1551f).

20 ORESTES and PYLADES now hide themselves and are not
noticed by the women until ORESTES speaks at 212.

22 The prevailing meter of the Parodos is the lyric iambics so
frequent in *Agamemnon*. The CHORUS consists of slave-
women of the house, who have come there as prisoners
of war (75f); they are sympathetic to ELECTRA.

23 It was usual for Greek mourners to tear their cheeks and
beat their heads as they lamented for the dead. Passionate
mourning was thought to be particularly characteristic of
Orientals (see 423f); it is not specifically stated that these
slave-women are Trojan prisoners, but the inference is not
unnatural.

11

loud in my grief resounds the rending of my robes,
the robes that veil my bosom; far from mirth   30
the disaster with which they are stricken.

ANTISTROPHE 1

For shrill, making the hair to stand on end,
the dream-prophet of the house, in sleep breathing anger,
uttered a midnight shriek
of terror from the heart of the palace   35
in grievous assault upon the women's chambers.
And interpreters of those dreams,
for whose rightness the gods stand surety, cried out
that those below the earth make angry complaint   40
and harbor wrath against the killers.

STROPHE 2

Such is the graceless grace to ward off harm—
O Mother Earth!—
that she has sent me to compass,   45
she the godless woman. But I am afraid
to let this word fall from my lips.
For what payment can atone for blood spilt upon the ground?
Ah, hearth of utter misery!
Ah, destruction of the house!   50
Sunless, hateful to mankind
is the darkness that shrouds the house
through the death of its master.

---

32 The cry was, in fact, uttered by CLYTEMNESTRA (535); the
    "dream-prophet" is the Daimon of the house, the personified
    curse upon it, who has caused her dream.

37 These interpreters are the domestic prophets mentioned
    also in *Agam.* 409.

44 As libations were poured onto the ground, the invocation
    of the Earth is natural.

47 *this word*: the prayer with which the pourer would normally
    accompany the libation (cf. ELECTRA's words at 87f).

48 That blood once spilt can never be atoned for is a theme
    that recurs again and again in the *Oresteia* (cf. *Agam.* 1017).

ANTISTROPHE 2

And the awe that once irresistible, invincible, not to be with-
    stood,   55
passed through the ear and mind of the people
now stands far away; and fear
is rife. Among mortals
success is a god and more than a god.   60
But the balance of justice is swift
to visit some beneath the light of day;
another fate awaits those that linger
in the twilight, a fate of woe;
and others night ineffectual enshrouds.   65

STROPHE 3

Because of blood drained by the fostering earth
the vengeful gore stands clotted, and will not dissolve away.
Calamity, inflicting grievous pain, keeps
the guilty man forever infected with an all-destroying sick-   70
    ness.

ANTISTROPHE 3

For him that has violated a bridal bower there is no
remedy; and though all streams flow
in one channel to cleanse the blood
from a polluted hand, they speed their course in vain.

EPODE

But as for me—since a constraint that beset my city   75
has been laid on me by the gods; for from the house
of my father they led me to a fate
of servitude—things just and things unjust

. . . . . .

---

61   The text is corrupt, the sense wholly uncertain. If the
emendation I have translated could be accepted, the sense
would presumably be that the avenging hand of Justice
strikes some during their lifetime, others only at the very
end of it, and others only in the underworld.

71   The sense is that just as virginity once lost cannot be
recovered, neither can the guilt of murder be washed away.

79   The text here is hopelessly corrupt.

must I approve, mastering the bitter   80
repugnance that is in my mind. And I weep behind my sleeve
for the hapless fortunes of my masters,
chilled by secret grief.

ELECTRA You servant women, who set the house in order,
since you are here in this supplication   85
to attend me, give me your counsel in this matter!
What am I to say while I pour these funeral offerings?
What wise words may I utter, what prayer may I make to my
    father? *1st Libation goes to Zeus + Hera*
Am I to say I bring them from a loving wife to a loved
husband, when I bring them from my mother?   90
That I dare not do; and I do not know what I can say
as I pour this libation on my father's tomb.
Shall I speak the words men are accustomed to speak,
"Grant in return equal benefits to those who send
these funeral honors"—yes, a gift deserving fair return!   95
Or must I in silence and dishonor, even as my father
perished, pour them forth for the earth to drink,
and retrace my steps, like one who has thrown out refuse,
hurling the vessel from me with averted eyes?
Share my responsibility, dear women, in deciding this;   100
for we share the hatred that we cherish in the house;
do not hide your counsel in your hearts through fear of any!
For the fated hour awaits both the free man
and him who is made subject by another's might.
Tell me, if you have any advice better than this!   105

A WHOLE ORDER IS DESTROYED
CONVENTION IS IMPOSSIBLE, DESPERATE IRONY

---

98   After throwing away refuse, the Greeks would turn away
     without looking around for fear that the malignant powers
     might be provoked by such an action.

103 The CHORUS, being slaves, may be unwilling to take the
     responsibility for offering advice. ELECTRA tries to overcome
     this feeling by reminding them that slave and free alike
     cannot escape their fate.

CHORUS *I revere your father's tomb as though it were
an altar;
and I will tell you, since you so order me, the thought that
comes from my heart.*

ELECTRA *Tell it me, even as you have voiced your
reverence for my father's grave.*

CHORUS *Speak, as you pour, words good for the loyal.*

ELECTRA *And to which among my friends am I to give
that title?*   110

CHORUS *First to yourself and to whoever hates
Aegisthus.*

ELECTRA *Then is it for myself and you that I must say
this prayer?*

CHORUS *You yourself learn the answer and then explain
it!*

ELECTRA *What other, then, must I add to this company?*

CHORUS *Remember Orestes, absent though he is.*   115

ELECTRA *Well said! Excellently have you instructed me.*

CHORUS *Then to those guilty of the murder, with
mindful heart . . .*

---

106 Dialogue lines belonging to the CHORUS, like those in this
scene, were spoken by its leader, the Coryphaeus.

108 This form of dialogue, called *stichomythia*, in which each
speaker utters one or two lines at a time, is characterized by
extreme stiffness and formality. Here the Coryphaeus gradu-
ally convinces ELECTRA to accompany the libation with a
prayer very different from that which CLYTEMNESTRA would
have wished. For the original audience, who believed strongly
in the efficacy of prayer and in the power of the dead to
influence events on earth, the matter had real importance.

111 *Aegisthus*: pronounce *Ee·gis'·thus.*

ELECTRA   What shall I say? Prescribe the form, instruct
my inexperience!

CHORUS   Pray that there may come to them some god or
mortal. . .

ELECTRA   Do you mean a judge or one who does justice?   120

CHORUS   Express it plainly—one who shall take life
for life!

ELECTRA   And can I ask this of the gods without
impiety?

CHORUS   Surely you can ask them to pay back an enemy
with evil!

A MORAL CODE (handwritten left margin)

ELECTRA   Mightiest herald of things above and things
below   165
help me, Hermes of the earth! Call upon
the deities below the earth to hear my prayers,   125
those who watch over your father's house.
And call upon the Earth herself, on her who brings forth
all things
and when she has nurtured them receives again their
increase.
And as I pour this lustral water for the dead

2nd libation to the Heroes - the particular shrines located around Greece. Not Olympians (handwritten left margin)

---

123   It was a truism of early Greek popular morality that one
should do good to one's friends and harm to one's enemies.
Thus the respected Solon prays, "May I taste sweet in the
mouths of my friends, bitter in those of my enemies; may I
be respected by friends and feared by foes."

165   Hermes was the patron of heralds (cf. *Agam.* 514), as well
as the intermediary between the world above and the world
below. This is line 165 in the manuscript, but is generally
believed to belong here.

126   See note on 1.

129   The sprinkling of lustral water preceded every sacrifice, including a libation (cf. *Agam.* 1037).

I call upon my father, and say, "Take pity on me, 130
and kindle in our house the dear light that is Orestes!"
For now are we, as it were, vagrants, sold
by our mother, who has got in exchange as husband
Aegisthus, him who is guilty of your murder.
I live the life of a slave; and from his possessions 135
Orestes is an exile; and they in their arrogance
enjoy great luxury amid the profits of your labor.
And that Orestes may come here with happy fortune
I pray to you. Do you hear me, father,
and for me, grant that I may be more right-minded by far 140
than my mother, and in my acts more innocent.
For us I utter this prayer; and for our enemies
I pray that one may appear to avenge you, father,
and that the killers may in justice pay with life for life.
This I interpose in the middle of my prayer for good, 145
against them uttering that prayer for evil.
But for us convey upward good fortune,
by grace of the gods and earth and justice triumphant!
Such are my prayers, and after them I pour forth these
        offerings.
And custom bids that you crown them with flowers of
        lamentation, 150
giving voice to the paean for the dead. *PARADOX AGAIN*

CHORUS Shed a plashing tear, lost
for our lost master,

---

145 This is evidently a ritual formula, designed to make it quite
     clear to the deity that the evil prayed for was only for the
     speaker's enemies, whereas the good was for the speaker's
     friends.

151 A paean is a kind of hymn, originally sung in honor of
     Apollo and having cheerful associations. Thus to speak of a
     "paean for the dead" conveys a kind of paradox.

152 The CHORUS sings a short lyric stanza without strophic
     responsion; the meter is iambic mixed with the dochmiacs

upon this bulwark of evil,
this loathed pollution, averting what is good,   155
that is the libation we have poured. Hear me, majesty!
Hear me, king, from your gloom-enshrouded spirit!
Ah, what man shall come, mighty with the spear,   160
deliverer of the house,
brandishing in his hands the Scythian armament,
and in close combat wielding weapons whose haft he grasps?

> ELECTRA Now my father has received the libations
> which the earth has drunk.

> ELECTRA notices a lock of hair on the tomb.

But here is news; share it with me!   166

> CHORUS Speak; my heart is dancing with alarm.

> ELECTRA I see here upon the tomb a severed lock.

> CHORUS To what man or what deep-girdled maiden can
> it belong?

> ELECTRA That is easy for anyone to guess.   170

> CHORUS Then may my old age learn from your youth?

so often found in lyrics that express emotional agitation. The rhythm of the dochmiac meter is well conveyed by Jebb's mnemonic: "Thĕ wīse kān-gărōos/Rĕsēnt lēath-ĕr shōes."

154 The text is uncertain. If the interpretation here adopted is correct, the CHORUS, despite ELECTRA's attempt to alter the effect of CLYTEMNESTRA's libation by accompanying it with her own prayer, still refers to the offering as though it were an instrument of CLYTEMNESTRA's purpose.

162 The Scythians, who inhabited the country between the Carpathians and the River Don, were famous archers.

168 ELECTRA notices the lock referred to by ORESTES in the Prologue (see note on 6). Only a close relation would make such an offering to the dead.

171 A stereotyped form of expression; it recurs at *The Suppliants* 361.

ELECTRA   There is none but I that could have shorn it.

CHORUS   Yes, for they to whom it fell to offer hair in mourning are his enemies.

ELECTRA   Yes, to the eye it seems very like . . .

CHORUS   Like whose hair? That is what I wish to know.   175

ELECTRA   It is very like my own to look upon.

CHORUS   Can it then be a secret offering of Orestes?

ELECTRA   It seems very like his locks.

CHORUS   And how has he dared to come here?

ELECTRA   He has sent a shorn lock in honor of his father.   180

CHORUS   In your words lies yet greater cause for tears,
to think that his foot shall never more tread this soil.

ELECTRA   To my heart also rises a wave
of bitterness, and I am pierced as though an arrow had
        transfixed me;
and from my thirsty eyes there pour,   185
uncontrollable, the drops of a stormy flood,
as I look upon this lock. For how can I suppose
that any other in the city is the owner of this hair?
Why, no, it was not his murderess who shore it,
my mother, whose heart   190
is all unmotherly toward her children.
For me to assent outright,
and say this adornment comes from the dearest
of mortals to me, Orestes . . . but hope is flattering me!

---

181   Both the Coryphaeus and ELECTRA are saddened by the thought that even if the lock belonged to ORESTES, its presence on the tomb does not prove that he came in person to Argos.

185   The eyes are called "thirsty" because they are thought of as longing for moisture and, therefore, shedding tears.

Ah, if it had only sense and language, like a messenger,   195
so that I was not tossed this way and that in two minds,
but either I knew for certain that I must reject this lock,
supposing it were cut from an enemy's head,
or it was kin to me and could share my grief,
adorning this tomb and honoring my father!   200
But the gods on whom we call know well
by what tempests we, like sailors,
are buffeted; and if we are fated to find safety,
from a small seed a mighty trunk may come.

    She notices the footprints.

Yes, and here are tracks, a second indication,   205
the tracks of feet matching each other and resembling mine.
Yes, here are two outlines of feet,
his own and those of a fellow traveler.
The heels and the marks of the tendons in their measure-
    ments agree with my own prints.   210
I am in torment, and my reason is confounded!

    ORESTES and PYLADES emerge from their hiding
    place.

---

205   The recognition of the footprints is mercilessly ridiculed by
Euripides in his *Electra* (518f; see Introduction, page 5).
There is no good reason to doubt the genuineness of the footprint episode. In the *Odyssey* Menelaus remarks that the
hands and feet of Telemachus resemble those of his father
Odysseus (4, 149). Since the theory that the beauty of the
body depended on its proportions was known to Greek
sculptors as early as the first half of the fifth century, relatives might very well be thought to resemble each other in
the proportions of their hands and feet. Further, the footprints provide ELECTRA and the CHORUS with an indication
of ORESTES' presence distinctly more reliable than the lock.
A lock, as they are quick to remember, might have been sent
to Argos from abroad, but not a footprint.

ORESTES   Pray, as you make acknowledgment to the gods
that your prayers have been fulfilled, that in the future
also you may fare well!

ELECTRA   Why, what fortune now do the gods allot me?

ORESTES   You have come to the sight of what you have
long prayed to look on.   215

ELECTRA   And whom among men do you know that
I call for?

ORESTES   I know that you make much of the name of
Orestes.

ELECTRA   And why then have I found an answer to my
prayer?

ORESTES   I am he; look for none closer to you than I!

ELECTRA   Why, are you weaving some snare against me,
stranger?   220

ORESTES   If so, I am hatching a plot against myself.

ELECTRA   Would you make sport of my misfortunes?

ORESTES   Of my own too, if I make sport of yours.

COMPARABLE STICHO TO AGA MEETING CLYTA.

ELECTRA   Then am I to address you as Orestes?

ORESTES   Why, you see my very self, and find me hard to
recognize;   225
yet when you had seen the hair I had cut off in mourning,
you were excited, and thought you saw me;
and when you were scanning the traces of my footprints

· · · · · ·

He offers her the lock.   *FOLK TALE: RIGHT OUT OF SSPEARE.*

Put the lock to the place from which I cut it,
and see how like is your brother's head to your own!   230

He offers her the garment.

Look on this piece of weaving, the work of your hand,

on the strokes of the batten, and the picture of the beasts
    upon it!
Contain yourself! Do not lose your wits for joy,
for I know that those closest to us are hateful to us.

ELECTRA O best beloved darling of your father's house,   235
O hope, much wept for, of seed that can preserve,
trusting in your prowess you shall win back the house of
    your father.
O joy-giving presence that has four characters
for me! For I must address
you as my father, and to you falls the love   240
I should bear my mother—her I most justly hate—
and that I bore the sister who was ruthlessly smitten.
And you have been a brother true to me, you who showed
    me due regard.
Only may Power and Justice, and Zeus the third,
mightiest of all, be on your side!   245

ORESTES Zeus, Zeus, be witness of these doings!
And look upon the orphan brood of the father eagle,

---

235 The word rendered by "darling" is a lover's word, found
in high poetry but also in comedy.

237 *trusting . . . prowess*: this phrase echoes a familiar Homeric
expression. What follows (238f) is an obvious reminiscence
of Andromache's great speech in the sixth book of the *Iliad*;
Andromache, who has lost her parents and brothers, says,
"Hector, you are my father and my lady mother, you are my
brother and you are my husband."

242 IPHIGENEIA. In Homer, Agamemnon has three daughters—
Chrysothemis, Laodice, and Iphianassa. Of these names, only
Chrysothemis occurs in tragedy (Sophocles' *Electra*).

244 The third libation at banquets was poured in honor of Zeus
the Preserver, and he was sometimes referred to as "Zeus
the Third Preserver" (cf. *Agam.* 1385, with my note; *Eum.*
758).

247 The eagle was the bird of Zeus.

of him who perished in the coils and meshes
of a dread viper! Bereft of their father
they are oppressed by starving famine; for they are not yet
    full grown,   250
so as to bring a quarry like their father's to the nest.
Even thus may I and Electra here
be seen by you, children robbed of our father,
both alike exiles from our home.
Now if you cause to perish these nestlings of a father   255
who made sacrifice and did you great honor, how
shall you get the honor of rich banquets from such a hand
    as his?
If you cause the eagle's brood to perish, you will no more
be able to send signs to men that they will trust;
and if this stem of royalty becomes all withered,   260
it will no more serve your altars on the days when oxen are
    slaughtered.
Rescue and raise it from humble state to greatness,
our house, low though now it seems to lie.

CHORUS O children, O preservers of your father's hearth,
be silent that none may observe you   265
and for the sake of talking report all this
to those in power; them may I one day see
perish in the pitchy ooze of the flame!

ORESTES Never shall I be betrayed by Loxias' mighty

---

258   The eagle was also important in augury; compare the portent
     of the eagles in the Parodos of *Agam.* 110f.

264   In scenes of conspiracy the leader of the CHORUS often has
     the function of reminding the conspirators of the danger of
     discovery.

267   A fragment of Aeschylus mentions the practice of covering
     people with pitch and then burning them alive.

269   *Loxias* is a name for Apollo, given him in his aspect as a

oracle, which commands me to pass through this danger, 270
raising many a loud cry and naming
chilly plagues to freeze my warm heart,
should I not take vengeance on those guilty of the murder,
after the same fashion bidding me take life for life,
driven to fury by the grievous loss of my possessions. 275
And with my own precious life, he said, I should pay
this debt, enduring many loathsome ills.
For as he revealed to mortals the means of mollifying
malignant powers below the earth, he spoke, naming these
      plagues—
leprous ulcers that mount upon the flesh with cruel fangs, 280
eating away its primal nature;
and a white down sprouting forth upon this infection.
And he spoke of other assaults of the Erinyes,
brought about by the shedding of my father's blood.
     . . . . . .
seeing . . . clear, though in the dark he directs his glance. 285
For the dark arrows of the infernal powers,
darted by kindred fallen who call for vengeance,

---

god of prophecy and thought to be connected with a word meaning "crooked." It thus refers to the deviousness of his oracles.

275 Note that both here and at 301 the need to recover his house and property is mentioned as one of ORESTES' motives.

276 Primitive and horrifying though the passage doubtless is, that is no reason for rejecting it as interpolated. Further, it is essential to the play; ORESTES must at this point lay heavy stress on the awful consequences of *not* killing his mother. The Erinyes were thought to afflict their victims with loathsome diseases (280–83) and madness (286–90). A person polluted by the shedding of a kinsman's blood was excluded from religious worship and social contact with others (291–94). The Erinyes were thought to suck their victims' blood (295–96); at *Eum.* 264–65, they themselves threaten ORESTES with this fate.

284 There is a gap in the text at this point; the object of the verb "seeing" in 285 is lost.

and madness and vain midnight fears
harass and torment and drive him from the city,
his body maimed by the brazen scourge.   290
And such men may have no part in the festal bowl
or in the pouring of drink-offering,
but are kept far from the altars by their father's unseen
wrath; and none may receive nor entertain such a one,
but he must perish at last honorless and friendless,   295
cruelly shriveled by a death that wastes him utterly away.
Such were the oracles; and must I not believe them?
Even if I lack belief, the deed must be done.
For many longings move to one end;
so do the god's command and my great sorrow for my father; 300
and moreover I am hard pressed by the want of my
        possessions,
not to leave the citizens of the most glorious city upon
        earth,
the overthrowers of Troy with noble hearts,
thus to be subject to a pair of women.
For his heart is a woman's; whether mine is, he shall soon
        know.   305

CHORUS   *Come, mighty Fates, by the will of Zeus*

---

302   This passage recalls the protest of the Chorus of Argive
      elders against having to submit to the rule of the usurpers
      in the final scene of *Agamemnon*. 305 recalls the moment
      during that scene when the Coryphaeus addresses AEGISTHUS
      as "Woman" (1625).

306   In *Prometheus*, where the possibility of Zeus's fall from
      power exists, the will of Zeus is not necessarily identical with
      fate (515f); but as long as Zeus reigns, his will and fate are
      the same. The philosophical problem of determinism had
      not at this time presented itself to the poets, and we must
      beware of supposing that they took either a determinist
      or an antideterminist view.

306– The lyric part of the conjuration scene is often called "The
478   Great Kommos"; *Kommos* means the "beating" of the head
      or breast by mourners and it denotes a scene in which the

CHORUS and actors sing alternate stanzas as they do here. This part of the scene is unique in tragedy, both in its form and in its content. To grasp its import it is necessary to remember that the poet assumes belief in the power of the dead to influence events on earth. It is all-important for ORESTES and ELECTRA to establish contact with the departed spirit of Agamemnon and to secure its aid in taking revenge upon the murderers. This simple but central fact has not proved easy for all modern minds to grasp. Many critics, including even the great scholar Wilamowitz, have tried to show that the great conjuration takes place in order to overcome the reluctance of ORESTES to commit the awful act of matricide. In order to strengthen the case for this theory, they have conjectured that lines 434–38 have been accidentally transposed and should come after 455; they would thus constitute the last of the lyric stanzas uttered in alternation by ORESTES, ELECTRA, and the CHORUS. There is no ground for supposing anything of the sort (see note on the passage in question). Nor is there anywhere any suggestion that ORESTES, like Hamlet, needs strengthening in his resolve; his long speech at 269 shows him fully determined and explains why. The great conjuration is directed not at the living but at the dead.

The conjuration scene consists of a lyric part (306–478) and a spoken part (479–509), in which the same ground is gone over in the less emotional and more explicit fashion proper to spoken dialogue. We may compare the division of the Cassandra scene of *Agamemnon* into a lyric and a spoken part. In the lyric half ORESTES, ELECTRA, and the CHORUS sing lyric stanzas in alternation, with marching anapests by the CHORUS at regular intervals. The responsion of the lyric stanzas is unique; instead of each strophe being followed by the corresponding antistrophe, the greater part of the scene shows a curious kind of interlacing responsion between stanzas placed at intervals from each other. The pattern is as follows:

I. 306–14 Marching anapests of CHORUS
    315–22 Strophe 1 (ORESTES)
    323–31 Strophe 2 (CHORUS)

KOMMOS — to draw forth the powers of grievances.

The introductory anapests serve as a transition. The first section of the lyric scene (315–423), the dirge over the tomb, consists of six strophes with their antistrophes arranged to form four triads, separated from one another by marching anapaests of the CHORUS; the meter is for the most part aeolic mixed with iambic. The second section (424–55), the conjuration proper, consists of three strophic pairs in irregular response followed by a strophe and antistrophe in which the two actors sing one line each and the CHORUS the rest. The meter of this section is iambic; it contains no marching anapests, not even at its beginning or end. The third section of the lyric scene consists of a short stanza by the CHORUS in Aeolic meter, not forming part of the Kommos proper, but containing the comment of the CHORUS on what has gone before. Marching anapests of the CHORUS of 476–78 round off the first section of the conjuration scene.

accomplish, even by the way
that Justice now moves to tread!
"For hateful word let hateful
word be paid"; as she demands her due   310
loud cries the voice of Justice;
"for murderous stroke let murderous
stroke atone." "Let the doer suffer";
so goes a saying three times ancient.

STROPHE 1

ORESTES   *Father, who fathered us to woe,*   315
what word or act
can I succeed in wafting to you from above
where you lie in your resting place?
Over against the realm of darkness stands the realm of light;
yet none the less the lament   320
that brings them honor is a joy
for the Atreidae who lie before the palace.

STROPHE 2

CHORUS   *My son, the dead man's mind is not subdued*
by the fire's ravening jaw;   325

---

309   The words of the CHORUS recall the terms in which the
Chorus of *Agamemnon* warned CLYTEMNESTRA of the truth
of this fundamental principle of Aeschylean justice (1563f).

315   Before all else ORESTES must establish communication with
his father; this can be effected by lamenting at his tomb.
The world of the dead is separate from the world of the
living, but the dead take pleasure in ritual lamentation.

322   *Atreidae:* pronounce Ă·*try*´·*dee.*
     Agamemnon's tomb, visible in the center of the stage,
stands before the palace, whose doors will later open. Likewise, Pindar speaks of the dead kings of Cyrene as being
buried "before the palace" (*Pythian* V. 96).

324   The doctrine here enunciated by the CHORUS is vital to the
understanding of the whole conjuration. "The punisher"

28

but late in time he shows his anger.
The dead is lamented,
and the punisher is revealed;
and the lament due to fathers
and begetters hunts down the guilty one, 330
when raised full loud and strong.

ANTISTROPHE 1

ELECTRA *Hear now, O father, as in turn*
we voice our grief with many tears!
It is your two children who bewail you
in a dirge over your tomb! 335
Your tomb has received them as suppliants
and as exiles alike.
What is there here of good? What here is free from ill?
Is not ruin still unconquered?

CHORUS *But even though things are thus, a god, if he*
    will,
may yet cause us to utter cries of more auspicious note; 340
and instead of lamentations by the grave
the paean in the royal halls
may bring back the well-loved mixing bowl of new wine.

---

(328) is the personified curse, or perhaps the dead man's spirit, whom the lament will arouse to vengeance.

336 Cf. 254, where ORESTES claims that he and ELECTRA are both exiles. For a Greek, exile involved the loss of one's rights, so that even though ELECTRA had not left Argos she can still be called an exile. The expression used implies that the tomb is compared to an altar, where suppliants take refuge; it has been compared to one by the CHORUS at 106, and the poet Simonides said of the heroic dead at Thermopylae, "Their tomb is an altar."

343 On the paean, see note on 151. There is probably allusion to the mixing bowl of new wine that was used at funerals or feasts.

29

STROPHE 3

ORESTES *Would that beneath Ilium*   345
pierced by the spear of one of the Lycians,
father, you had been slain!
You would have left glory in your halls,
and for your children a life
that would have made men turn to view them
in their walks abroad;   350
and you would have occupied a high-heaped
tomb in a land beyond the sea,
a fate your house could easily have borne.

ANTISTROPHE 2

CHORUS *Dear to the dear ones who nobly fell at Troy,*
preeminent below the earth   355
as a king of august majesty,
and minister of the mighty
rulers there below!

---

346 *Lycians:* pronounce *Licé·ïans.*

The Lycians are mentioned presumably because they, under their leaders Sarpedon and Glaucus, were the bravest allies of the Trojans. ORESTES' whole speech is modeled on one made by Achilles in *The Odyssey* (24. 30f). He speaks in Hades to Agamemnon and says he wishes that Agamemnon had been killed before Troy instead of meeting his death as he did.

354 Some scholars have wanted to emend the text because it seems to imply that Agamemnon's status in Hades was affected by the manner of his death, a notion the critics finds surprising. But two passages in *The Odyssey* (11. 388; 24. 20) might be held to imply this; his ghost is described as "sorrowful," and it is surrounded by the souls, not of those who fell at Troy, but of those who fell in the ambush in which he perished. The same notion governs Virgil's portraits of the dead in the underworld (*Aeneid* 6. 479f).

For you were a king, while you lived, 360
over those that fulfilled their mortal lot,
with your might and with your man-controlling scepter.

ANTISTROPHE 3

ELECTRA *Not even beneath Troy's*
walls, father, would I have had you perish,
and with the rest of the host that perished by the spear 365
be buried by Scamander's stream!
But would that first your slayers
had been brought low in such a fashion
that far off men might have learned 370
of their deadly fate,
even men with no part in these troubles!

CHORUS *All this is more precious than gold, my child.*
Greater than great good fortune, even that of the blessed,
are the things you speak of; for it is in your power.
But now—for the thud of this double 375
scourge strikes home!—our cause has champions
already below the earth, and those in power,
these hateful ones, have hands that are not clean;
and it is for you, his children, to act!

STROPHE 4

ORESTES *This pierces through to my ear* 380
like an arrow!
Zeus, Zeus, you who send up from below
late-avenging ruin
to the ruthless and reckless violence of men,
nonetheless the debts due to parents shall be discharged! 385

---

375 *double scourge:* the beating of both hands on the tomb.

376 The thought that "our cause has already its champions below the earth" is of course calculated to encourage the
avengers, as is the thought that the hands of their enemies
are stained with blood (cf. 66f with note).

382 The reference is to Hades, whom Aeschylus calls "the Zeus
below" (see note on 1).

STROPHE 5

CHORUS *May it be granted me to raise a piercing*
cry of triumph when the man
is smitten and the wife
perishes! For why do I hold back
what at all events hovers here
—and before my heart's prow　　　　　　　　　390
blows a cutting wind
of rage—my mind's rancorous hatred?

ANTISTROPHE 4

ELECTRA *And when shall the mighty*
Zeus lay his hand upon them—　　　　　　　395
ah, ah, severing their heads?
Grant an assurance to our land!
Justice from the unjust I demand!
Hear me, Earth and honored powers below!

CHORUS *But it is the law that drops of blood*　　　400
spilt on the ground demand further
bloodshed; for murder calls on the Erinys,
who from those who perished before
brings one ruin in another's wake.

STROPHE 6

ORESTES *Alas, sovereign powers of the world below!*　　405
Look on us, powerful curses of the dead!
Behold the remains of the Atreidae in their helplessness
cast out in dishonor from their home! Which way
is one to turn, Zeus?

---

386 This is the first mention of the idea that CLYTEMNESTRA
must be killed.

402 *Erinys:* pronounce E·*rine'·is.*

408 Those who try to make the play into a modern drama by
arguing that ORESTES hesitates to decide to kill his mother
invest this rhetorical question with a perplexity that is not
really there. ORESTES' determination is shown by his calling
upon the rulers of the underworld and the curses of the
dead (sometimes identified with the Erinyes, as at *Eum.*
417); it amounts to an appeal to Zeus for aid.

ANTISTROPHE 5

CHORUS *My heart is in turmoil once more,*   410
as I listen to this lament.
And now I am bereft of hope,
and my mind darkens
at these words as I hear them;
but when once more valiant confidence prevails,   415
hope removes my pain,
appearing before me in her beauty.

ANTISTROPHE 6

ELECTRA *What must we say to find the target? Must*
  we recount
the agonies we have suffered, yes, from our begetters?
She may try to fawn upon him, but there is no appease-
  ment;   420
for like a savage wolf, not to be cajoled
by my mother, is his wrath.

STROPHE 7

CHORUS *I beat an Arian dirge upon my breast, after*
  the fashion
of a Cissian wailing woman,
and with clenched fists and much spattering of blood   425

---

413   In moments of violent passion the *phrenes*, originally perhaps the lungs but believed to be the seat of thought, were
said to darken (cf. e.g., *The Iliad* 1. 103).

418   Cf. 315f; they have to establish communication with the
dead man's ghost and arouse it to indignation.

422   *Arian:* pronounce *Air′·ian.*
Here ends the dirge at the tomb, the first section of the
lyric part of the conjuration scene.

423   *Cissian:* pronounce *Siss′·ian.*
The CHORUS appears to be recalling its behavior during the
delivery of the Parodos (22f). "The Arians" was an old
name for the Medes, and Cissia was the district of Persia
in which lay Susa, the ancient capital; the Greeks associated
passionate lamentation with Orientals.

could you have seen once more and yet once more my arms
    stretched forth
from above, from on high, and while the ringing blows re-
    sounded
upon my battered, miserable head.

STROPHE 8

ELECTRA   Ah, ah, cruel,
reckless mother, in a cruel burial   430
a king without his people,
without his due of mourning
a husband you had the heart to bury unlamented!

STROPHE 9

ORESTES   All without honor he was, as you tell it.
But for my father's dishonoring she shall pay,   435
by the action of the gods,
and by the action of my hands.
Then may I perish, once I have slain her!

ANTISTROPHE 9

CHORUS   He was mutilated; I must tell you this;
and the doer was she who gave him this funeral,   440
striving to make his death
a burden on your life.

---

429   CLYTEMNESTRA had denied Agamemnon's body a proper burial (cf. *Agam.* 1551f).

434   This stanza is transposed to follow 455 by those who think the conjuration takes place to give ORESTES the strength to decide to kill his mother. They have mistaken the sense of 438, which they take to mean that once he has killed his mother, ORESTES no longer wishes to live. But in Greek poetry it is common to say, "May I die, once I have killed X," meaning simply that one would do anything if one could only kill X; the expression is of the type discussed in my note on *Agam.* 539 (cf. also *Agam.* 550). These words of ORESTES give no ground for supposing that he hesitates to obey Apollo's command.

439   Murderers used to mutilate the corpses of their victims to prevent their ghosts from pursuing them; they cut off the

34

Now you know the woes your father suffered, all without
    honor.

ANTISTROPHE 7

ELECTRA   You tell of my father's end; but I was far
    away,
dishonored, I that deserved a better fate!   445
Shut away in my chamber like a savage dog
I gave forth watery drops more readily than laughter,
as in my prison I poured out a lament of many tears.
Hear this and write it in your mind, father!   450

ANTISTROPHE 8

CHORUS   Write it; and let our words pass through
    your ears
with tranquil mind.
For these things are as we say;
yourself be passionate to hear the rest!
With wrath inflexible must you enter the struggle!   455

STROPHE 10

ORESTES   On you I call! Be with your dear ones, father!

ELECTRA   I join my voice to his, bathed in tears.

CHORUS   And this whole company echoes the call.
Come to the light, and hear us!
Be with us against our enemies!   460

ANTISTROPHE 10

ORESTES   Might shall clash with might, Justice with
    Justice.

ELECTRA   O ye gods, fulfill my prayer as Justice de-
    mands.

CHORUS   A shudder creeps over me as I hear the prayer!
Doom has long since been waiting;
and may it come to us as we pray for it!   465

---

    hands and feet of the victim, strung them on a rope, put
    the rope round his neck, and drew it under his armpits.

461 CLYTEMNESTRA, as avenger of Iphigeneia, and AEGISTHUS, as
    avenger of his brothers and sisters, each had a certain meas-

STROPHE 11

Ah, sorrow inbred in the race,
and bloody stroke
of ruin discordant!
Ah, woes lamentable, unbearable!
Ah, pain not to be quelled!   470

ANTISTROPHE 11

The house has a remedy for this,
a remedy of suppuration; not from others,
without, but from its own children
must it come, by means of cruel, bloody strife.
To the gods beneath the earth this hymn is sung!   475

Come, give ear, blessed ones below the earth,
to this prayer, and send help
readily to his children, so that they triumph!

ORESTES Father, who perished in unkingly fashion,
grant my prayer for the lordship of your house!   480

---

ure of justice on their side when they slew Agamemnon; so
of course has ORESTES when he comes to avenge his father.

466 This concluding strophe and antistrophe are not part of the
conjuration, which ends at 465, but comprise a brief comment by the CHORUS.

471 A suppurating wound was treated by the application of
"tents" or "pledgets" designed to catch the pus, a remedy
that was used only in desperate cases. In this case the "treatment" consists in the successive murders.

475 Hymns were normally sung to the Olympian gods of heaven,
so that the idea of a hymn to the gods of the underworld
conveys something of the grim travesty of a "paean of the
Erinyes" at *Agam.* 645.

476 The CHORUS rounds off the lyric part of the conjuration
scene with a final prayer for victory to the gods below.

479 ORESTES and ELECTRA now make their appeal to the ghost
in more explicit and less emotional fashion, using dialogue
instead of lyric meter and speaking instead of singing.

ELECTRA   I, too, have a like request for you—
that I may escape after having laid utter ruin on Aegisthus.

ORESTES   For thus you may get the banquets that are
       men's custom;
but if we fail, while others feast richly you shall go without
your due honor at the savory banquet of burnt offerings.   485

ELECTRA   And I shall bring you libations from my rich
       store,
wedding libations from my paternal home;
and first of all I shall do honor to this tomb.

ORESTES   O Earth, send up my father to survey the
       battle!

ELECTRA   O Persephassa, grant him beauteous victory!   490

ORESTES   Remember the bath in which you were
       murdered, father!

ELECTRA   Remember the new sort of covering they
       devised!

ORESTES   You were caught in fetters of no smith's
       working, father!

ELECTRA   And in the shroud of a vile plot!

ORESTES   Do these shameful words not rouse you,
       father?   495

ELECTRA   Do you not raise erect your beloved head?

ORESTES   Either send Justice to fight by your dear ones'
       side,

---

483   Compare this appeal to the simple self-interest of the ghost
       with the appeal to the self-interest of Zeus at 255f.

490   Persephassa is another name for Persephone.

491   ELECTRA echoes ORESTES' opening word, "remember"; this
       reinforces the effect of exact symmetry between the utter-
       ances of the two speakers that persists throughout this scene.

or grant that we in turn get a like grip on them,
if it is your will to atone for your defeat by victory.

ELECTRA   Hear also this last cry, father!   500
Look upon your nestlings here at your tomb,
and pity alike my woman's and his man's cry!

ORESTES   Do not wipe out this race of the Pelopidae!
For if we live you are not dead, even in death.
For children preserve a man's fame   505
after his death; like corks they hold up the net,
retaining the cord of flax that reaches up from the deep.

ELECTRA   Listen! It is for your sake that such laments
    are uttered,
and you yourself are preserved if you do honor to our words.

They retire from before the grave.

CHORUS   Indeed, there has been no fault in this your
    lengthy utterance;   510
making atonement to the tomb for the lament that was
    denied it;
and for the rest, since you are resolved to act,
do now the deed and make trial of your fortune.

---

503   Pelops was an ancestor of Agamemnon.

505–   These lines are attributed to Sophocles by an author who
507   quotes them; without them ORESTES and ELECTRA would
       deliver speeches of exactly equal length down to 509. They
       may well have been interpolated, as passages of sententious
       reflection often were.

510   The word translated "without flaw" implies that ORESTES
       and ELECTRA have correctly discharged the ritual in the
       invocation of the ghost.

512   These words have been misconstrued to imply that without
       the conjuration ORESTES would have been unable to sum-
       mon the resolve to kill his mother; in fact they imply noth-
       ing of the sort.

ORESTES It shall be so; but we are not deflected from
    our course if we inquire
why she sent libations, what calculation led her   515
to offer too late atonement for a hurt past cure.
But to the unconscious dead it was a poor solace
that she sent! I do not know to what to liken these
her gifts, but they are less than her offense.
For though a man pour out all he has in atonement for one   520
life taken—in vain is his labor; thus goes the saying.
If you know what I ask, tell it me; I wish to learn it.

CHORUS I know, my son, for I was there; by dreams
and fears that send men wandering in the night she was
    shaken,
so that she sent these libations, the godless woman.   525

ORESTES Do you know the nature of the dream, so that
    you can truly tell it?

CHORUS She thought she brought forth a snake,
    according to her own account.

ORESTES And where ends her story and where lies its
    consummation?

CHORUS She laid it to rest in swaddling clothes, as
    though it were a child.

ORESTES What food did it desire, the newborn
    monster?   530

---

520 Again the constantly repeated motive of the irrevocability
    of bloodshed (cf. 71f, etc.).

525 *the godless woman:* what the CHORUS called CLYTEMNESTRA
    in the Parodos (46).

527 In the *Oresteia* of the early lyric poet Stesichorus, Clytem-
    nestra dreamed of a snake. But it seems that there the
    snake symbolized, not ORESTES, but Agamemnon (see Intro-
    duction, page 2).

CHORUS *She herself offered it her breast in the dream.*

ORESTES *And how did her teat remain unwounded by the hateful creature?*

CHORUS *It did not, but with the milk it sucked a curd of blood.*

ORESTES *It is a vision of a man, no empty one.*

CHORUS *And in her sleep she screamed in terror.*   535
And many lamps that darkness had made blind
were kindled in the palace for the mistress' sake.
And then she sent these funeral libations,
hoping for a cure to cut away her distress.

ORESTES *Well, I pray to the earth here and to my father's tomb*   540
that this dream may be fulfilled for me;
and see, I interpret it so as to tally at all points.
For if the snake came from the same place as I
and lay among my swaddling clothes,
and opened its mouth about the breast that fed me,   545
and mingled the kindly milk with a curd of blood,
and she in terror cried out at the event,
it must come about, I say, that even as she fed the monstrous portent,
so must she die by violence, and it is I that turn into a snake
and slay her, as this dream announces.   550

CHORUS *I choose your reading of this prodigy.*
May it be so! But expound the rest to your friends,
bidding some take measures, and others refrain from action.

ORESTES *Simple is the telling. Electra must go inside;*

---

539   Cautery and excision were the two main methods of ancient chirurgery; the metaphor is from the latter (cf. *Agam.* 849–50).

551   Like the speech of the Coryphaeus at 510–13, this serves to dismiss one topic and pass on to the next.

and I bid you keep secret this covenant with me, 555
so that they who by cunning slew an honored hero
may be taken by cunning, perishing
in the same snare, as Loxias has declared,
the lord Apollo, a prophet never proved false in the past.
In the guise of a stranger, fully equipped, 560
I shall come with this man to the gate of the courtyard,
with Pylades, a stranger and a spear-friend to the house.
And we will both speak the dialect of Parnassus,
copying the sound of the Phocian tongue.
Suppose none of the doorkeepers with welcome in his mind 565
receives us (for indeed a spirit is visiting the house with
    evil):
we shall wait so that someone may put two and two together,
as he passes by the house, and say this:
"Why does Aegisthus shut out the suppliant at the gates,
if he is at home and knows the man is there?" 570
Well, if I cross the threshold of the courtyard gates

---

556 According to the usual story, told also by Sophocles in his
Electra (35f), Apollo had told ORESTES that he must kill
Agamemnon's murderers by guile, just as they had killed
their victim.

560 ORESTES can call himself a stranger because he has been
away so long.

562 *Spear-friend:* a term for "ally," the spear being for the
Greeks, as the sword was for us, the weapon *par excellence;*
but ORESTES uses the term because he will presently use
violence against his enemies.

563 This means PYLADES' home country, where ORESTES spent
his exile.

569 Hospitality to strangers and "suppliants" was a religious
duty whose neglect might bring punishment from Zeus
Xenios, Zeus the Lord of Host and Guest.

571 In accordance with the usual technique of tragedy, the poet

and find him on my father's throne,
or if he returns and then comes face to face with me,
be assured, before he can cast down his eyes,
before he can say, "Where does the stranger come from?" I
    shall strike him   575
dead, spitting him on my swift-moving weapon.
And the Erinys that has had no stint of blood
shall drink unmixed gore in a third potation.
So now, Electra, keep good watch inside the house;
that this may turn out just as we wish;   580
and you women I charge to be discreet in speech,
to be silent where it is needful and to say what fits the time.
And for the rest I pray my father here to look upon us,
making the battle with the sword go right for me.

STROPHE 1

CHORUS *Many are the terrors bred of earth,*   585

---

is deliberately leading his audience to expect things that will not happen. According to one version of the story, familiar from vase paintings, AEGISTHUS was surprised by ORESTES while seated on his father's throne and killed instantly.

573 The text is uncertain.

581 The request to the CHORUS for silence is common in tragic scenes of conspiracy.

585 The pattern, "There are many formidable things, but this is the most formidable" recalls the famous First Stasimon of Sophocles' *Antigone*, "Many things are formidable, and most of all is Man." Further, the stasimon conforms to a standard type of choral ode in which the situation in the play is compared with other situations in the mythological past. When Antigone is sentenced to be buried alive, the Chorus compares her fate with those of three imprisoned persons in the past (944f); when Medea in Euripides' play is about to kill her children, the Chorus compares her with Ino, who in madness killed her offspring (1282f). This stasimon is corrupt in places, and in some of these it is very hard to

dread and woeful,
and the embraces of the ocean teem
with monsters inimical to mortals;
and between earth and heaven there come into being
lights that shine by day; 590
and winged things and things that walk the earth can tell
also of the stormy wrath of whirlwinds.

ANTISTROPHE 1

But of the reckless pride
of a man who can tell, 595
or of the desperate passions
of women without scruple, fellows
of the spirits that wreak ruin among mortals?

Unions in wedlock
are perverted by the victory of shameless passion, mastering
    the female, 600
among beasts and men.

STROPHE 2

Let any know this whose wits are not
unstable, having learned
of the plot which the killer of her son
Thestius' reckless daughter

---

understand. It begins in trochaic meter, which later changes
to iambic.

"Earth, sea and sky have bred many formidable crea-
tures; but what is more formidable than men's pride and
woman's passion?" (594f).

590 *lights that shine by day:* lightning and, perhaps, meteors.
604 *Thestius:* pronounce *Thess'·ti·us.*

Alythaea, daughter of Thestius, was wife of Oeneus, king of
Calydon, and mother of the great hero Meleager. Soon after
Meleager's birth it was predicted that he would not survive
longer than a brand then burning on the fire, and Althaea
seized the brand and kept it carefully. After Meleager with

43

accomplished　　　　　　　　　　　　　　　　　　　　　605
a plot of burning in the fire,
she who consumed in flames the charred brand assigned to
　　　her son,
that was his fellow in age, from the cry
he uttered when he left his mother's womb,
and remained coeval throughout life　　　　　　　　　610
to the day determined by fate!

ANTISTROPHE 2

And there is another woman in legend fit for abomination,
the murderous Scylla,
who at the behest of enemies
did to death one dear to her,　　　　　　　　　　　　615
lured by the Cretan
necklace wrought of gold,
the gift of Minos;
deliberately she deprived
Nisus of his lock of immortality,
she the shameless one, as he drew breath in sleep;　　　620
and Hermes overtook him.

---

other heroes had slain the great boar sent by Artemis to
ravage the crops of Calydon, he gave the spoils to the virgin
huntress Atalanta; in consequence a quarrel started in which
Meleager killed his mother's two brothers. Althaea in fury
took the brand and hurled it on the fire, and Meleager's death
followed.

612–　*Scylla:* pronounce *Sil'·la.*

620　　Nisus, king of Megara, had a purple lock; while he kept this
　　　lock, he could not die. Minos, king of Crete, attacked
　　　Megara with a fleet; Scylla, daughter of Nisus, persuaded
　　　by the gift of a necklace (or, according to one version, she
　　　fell in love with Minos), cut off the lock. Megara fell
　　　to the Cretans, and Scylla was changed into the sea-monster
　　　who figures in *The Odyssey* (see note on *Agam.* 1233).

618　*Minos:* pronounce *Mie'·nos.*

622　*Hermes:* pronounce *Herm'·ēs.*

Turning toward the palace.

STROPHE 3

And since I have called to mind pitiless
afflictions, I add the tale of the hateful
marriage, an abomination for the house,   625
and the daring deeds plotted by a woman's mind.
Against your warrior husband,
against your husband like an enemy did you go,
honoring the hearth of the house that lacked warmth
the cowardly spear of a man that was no man.   630

ANTISTROPHE 3

And first among crimes comes that of Lemnos
in story, and the people lament for it
with execration; and each new horror
men liken to the woes of Lemnos.
And in pollution hateful to the gods   635
the race of men has vanished with dishonor.
For none reveres what the gods detest.
Which of these tales have I unjustly cited?

STROPHE 4

And near the lungs the sword
drives sharply home a piercing stroke   640
by the action of Justice, who in defiance of the right
has been trampled underfoot,

Hermes, the conductor of spirits to Hades, overtook Nisus, who had hoped to remain immortal.

629 This refers to Aegisthus. A hearth that had only a man like Aegisthus to light it (see *Agam.* 1435-36) lacked proper warmth; the spear of Aegisthus was cowardly, for he was no proper man (cf. *Agam.* 1625).

631 *Lemnos:* pronounce *Lemn'·nos.*

Moved by jealousy of some women captives from Thrace, the women of Lemnos massacred all the men on the island, except the king Thoas, who was smuggled to safety by his daughter Hypsipyle.

striking those who have transgressed against the whole
  majesty of Zeus,
in defiance of the right.   645

ANTISTROPHE 4

The anvil of justice is planted firm;
and fate the swordsmith fashions in advance her weapon.
But the child is brought to the house
of ancient murders,
to atone at last for the pollution brought by the famed,   650
the deep-designing Erinys.

The CHORUS retires; ORESTES goes up to the gateway.

ORESTES   Boy, boy! Hear my knocking at the courtyard
  gate!
Who is inside? Boy, boy, I say once more, who is at home?
A third time I call for someone to cross the house,   655
if Aegisthus permits that it give hospitality.

SLAVE   All right, I can hear you. From what land is the
  stranger? From what place?

---

646   For a similar metaphor, compare *Agam.* 1535.

648   "The child of ancient murders" refers not to ORESTES but
      to the new murder that will soon take place; for the meta-
      phor, compare 806 below.

651   The telling word "Erinys" is held back until the end of
      the stanza; compare *Agam.* 59, 749.

653   ORESTES has already told ELECTRA and the CHORUS (571f)
      that he will immediately attack if he finds AEGISTHUS at
      the door; the moment when he approaches the door is
      therefore one of high dramatic tension. But, as usual, the
      poet has led the audience to expect things that actually
      turn out differently.

657   The SLAVE's words echo the traditional Homeric question to
      a stranger.

ORESTES Announce me to the masters of the house,
to whom I come bringing news;
and make haste, for Night's dusky chariot   660
is speeding on, and already it is time for travelers to drop
anchor in the hospitable houses of their hosts.
Let there come from the house some person in authority,
a lady, mistress of the place . . . but it would be fitter that
    a man should come.
For the respect one owes a woman in conversation obscures 665
one's words; a man can speak with confidence
to a man and make his meaning clear.

    Enter CLYTEMNESTRA.

CLYTEMNESTRA Strangers, say if there is anything you
    need! For we have
all that is fitting for this house;
hot baths, and bedding that charms away   670
fatigue, and the presence of honest eyes.
But if there is need for action that requires more counsel,
this is work for men, to whom we will impart it.

ORESTES I am a foreigner from Daulis among the
    Phocians
and as I traveled carrying my own pack   675
toward Argos—it is here that I have ended my journey—
a stranger met me and spoke to me,

---

664 ORESTES would naturally prefer to settle with AEGISTHUS
before being confronted with his mother.

668 Clytemnestra: pronounce Klīt·em·nes'·tra.

670 The sinister irony of these lines is manifest; the mention
of "hot baths" can hardly be an accident. Naturally this
irony is the poet's, directed toward the audience, not that
of CLYTEMNESTRA herself.

672 Compare Agam. 1608-9, 1614; AEGISTHUS planned the murder.

674 Daulis: pronounce Dor'·lis; Phocians: pronounce Fo'·shuns.

after asking me my errand and telling me his,
Strophius the Phocian; for as we talked I learned his name.
"Since in any case, stranger, you are going to Argos,   680
remember in all honesty, and tell his parents
that Orestes is dead; by no means forget.
To bring him home—if this is the prevailing wish of his own
    people
or to bury him in the land of his exile, an alien guest for all
    time—
these are the instructions you must convey back to us.   685
For now the sides of an urn of bronze
enclose the ashes of a man we have well bewailed."
So much I hear and I have told you. And if I happen
to be addressing those in authority, to whom it pertains,
I do not know; but it is proper that his parent know the
    truth.   690

CLYTEMNESTRA   Ah me! Your tale is of our utter ruin!
O curse upon this house, that we wrestle with in vain,
how far your vision ranges! Even what was well bestowed out
    of the way
you with your well-aimed arrows from afar bring down,
and strip me, in my misery, bare of friends!   695
And now—for Orestes kept good counsel,
keeping his foot outside the mire of ruin
now the hope that existed in the house as medicine

---

679   Father of PYLADES; compare *Agam.* 88of.

691   It is not safe to assume that the emotion CLYTEMNESTRA
      expresses is wholly false. But it is clear from her answer to
      ORESTES at 707f that her sorrow at the report of his death
      is greatly lessened by the thought that now she and
      AEGISTHUS are safe; the speech of the NURSE (734) with
      its spontaneous expression of unmixed grief throws this fact
      into strong relief.

698   When criminals were condemned to death in Athens, they
      were entered in the register as "present" or as "absent"

against the evil revelry you must write down as present and
  awaiting death.

ORESTES For my part, my hosts being so prosperous   700
I should have wished it were on account of good news
that I had become known to them and had been entertained;
  for where
is good will greater than between host and guest?
But piety made it seem wrong to me
not to fulfill such an office for Orestes' friends,   705
when I had given my promise and become your guest.

CLYTEMNESTRA I say that nonetheless you shall receive
  your due,
nor shall you be the less a friend to the house;
another might as well have come to bring this news.
But it is time that strangers who have spent the day   ·   710
on a long journey should get their proper entertainment!
Take him to the house's guest-chambers for men
and also these followers and fellow travelers,
and there let them have the treatment that befits this house;
and I charge you to act as one who will be held to strict
  account.   715
But we shall impart this to the ruler of the house
and we shall have no lack of friends
when we take counsel touching this event.

---

because only if they were present could the sentence be
carried out. If the interpretation I have adopted is correct,
the passage alludes to this fact; but this explanation is not
certain.

700 Messengers who brought good news commonly received a
rich reward, and tragic messenger scenes frequently contain
allusions to this fact.

713 ORESTES and PYLADES will have been accompanied by silent
slaves carrying their baggage.

716 Compare 672–73 with note.

Exit CLYTEMNESTRA followed by the others.

CHORUS *So be it, loyal handmaids of the house;*
when shall we display   720
the strength of our voices in honor of Orestes?
O sovereign Earth and sovereign mound
of the barrow that now lies
over the body of the master of the fleet, the king,
now give ear to us, now give us aid!   725
For now it is the time for guileful Persuasion
to enter the arena on his side, and for Hermes of the Earth
and of the Night to watch over this
contest of the deadly sword!

The stranger, it seems, is working some mischief!   730

---

719 The scene is separated from the next one by a brief passage
      of marching anapests chanted by the CHORUS; for this use
      of marching anapests, compare *Agam.* 783f, 1331f; also
      above, 306f.

727 For Hermes of the Earth, compare 1 with note; Hermes is
      also the god of thieves, who traditionally operate at night,
      and by Apollo's command ORESTES is employing guile to
      carry out his act of vengeance.

731f (See Introduction, page 7.) The NURSE, with her chatter
      about infants and their habits, affords the sharpest contrast
      to the dignity of all other Aeschylean characters. The only
      other humble character in Greek tragedy whose talk is char-
      acteristic of his station is the Guard in Sophocles' *Antigone*;
      no Euripidean nurse or slave is like this. Not that the
      NURSE's language is in any way like that of comedy; it is
      not its colloquialism but its reference to familiar and
      untragic matters that is surprising. In *The Iliad* (9. 490–91)
      Achilles' old tutor, Phoenix, refers similarly to the infantile
      habits of his former charge, and in *The Odyssey* (19. 363)
      Odysseus' old nurse, Eurycleia, laments similarly over her
      troubled life. The unfeigned sorrow of the talkative old
      woman supplies an effective contrast to the way in which
      CLYTEMNESTRA has received the news of her son's death.

Enter the NURSE.

But *I* see here Orestes' nurse in tears.
Where are you on your way to, Cilissa, that, that you are at
    the gate of the house?
grief is your unhired fellow traveler.

NURSE   The mistress bids me summon Aegisthus for the
    strangers
with all speed, so that unmistakably,   735
as man from man, he may come and learn
this story they have just reported. To the servants
she assumed a look of sorrow, hiding inside her eyes
the mirth she felt at work accomplished well
for her—but for this house things are altogether ill,   740
made so by the message which the strangers have rendered
    clearly.
Indeed his heart will be gladdened by the hearing,
once he learns the news. O woe is me!
For the ancient woes blended together
in this house of Atreus were hard to bear,   745

Also, by an effective stroke of tragic irony, the harmless
NURSE has a decisive effect upon the action, for the Coryph-
aeus makes her disobey CLYTEMNESTRA's orders and tell
AEGISTHUS to come without his bodyguard.

730f This speech is in trimeters and is spoken by the Coryphaeus,
like the rest of the dialogue with the NURSE. The Coryphaeus
infers that ORESTES is already getting to work.

732 *Cilissa:* pronounce *Sy·liss'·sa:* "Cilician woman." Many
slaves in Greece bore names that expressed their racial
origins; thus in the New Comedy "Getas" and "Syrus" are
common names for slaves. Stesichorus and Pindar (see Introduction, p. 2) had given the Nurse the heroic names
Laodameia and Arsinoe.

733 For the mode of expression, compare *Agam.* 979.

744 For the metaphor, compare *Agam.* 1395–98.

745 *Atreus:* pronounce *Ayt'·ruse.*

and afflicted the heart within my breast;
but never have I endured such agony as this!
For my other sorrows I bore patiently;
but my dear Orestes, for whom I wore away my life,
whom I reared up after I received him from his mother   750

• • • • • •

and of loud commands that set me moving in the night,
and I bore many labors without profit to myself—
for the unreasoning thing has to be nursed
as though it were an animal—how else?—according to its
    humor.
For a child still in swaddling clothes does not tell you   755
whether it is hungry, or maybe thirsty, or wants to make
    water;
and the infant stomach must have its own way.
To guess at these needs I had to be a prophet, and often, I
    know,
did my prophecy prove false, I who washed the child's swad-
    dling clothes;
and the offices of washerwoman and nurse were combined.   760
These two handicrafts were mine
when I received Orestes for his father;
and now, alas, they tell me of his death,
and I go to fetch that man who is the ruin
of this house, and gladly will he learn this story.   765

CHORUS   How then does she bid him come attended?

NURSE   What do you mean by "how"? Speak again, so
    that I can understand you better.

CHORUS   I mean, does she say with his guards or alone?

NURSE   She bids him bring the spearmen who attend
    him.

---

750   Something is certainly missing after 750; how much is quite
    uncertain. Line 750 implies that the NURSE cared for him
    from the moment he came into the world, as we can see
    from Odyssey 19. 353, whose language is plainly echoed here.

CHORUS *Then do not yourself give the news to our*
        detested ruler;   770
but tell him to come alone, to hear without fear the news
as soon as possible, and with rejoicing heart;
it rests with the messenger to put a crooked statement
    straight.

NURSE *But are you sane? After the message they have*
       brought?

CHORUS *But suppose Zeus should some day make to*
        change the wind   775
that blows us ill?

NURSE *What do you mean? Orestes, the hope of the*
       house, is gone.

CHORUS *Not yet; even a poor prophet could guess*
        that.

NURSE *What are you saying? Have you some knowl-*
       edge beyond
what has been told?

CHORUS *Go, take the message, do as you are ordered!*
The gods are caring for whatever is their care.   780

NURSE *Well, I will go and do as you say in this;*
and with the gods' granting may all turn out as well as maybe!

STROPHE 1

CHORUS *Now in answer to my prayer, Zeus,*
father of the Olympian gods,

---

780 Compare *Agam.* 974.

783 This ode is one of the most difficult in all Greek tragedy;
     its text is exceedingly corrupt, and in several places it cannot
     be restored with any real certainty. It consists of three
     strophes and antistrophes, whose prevailing meter is trochaic;
     between each strophe and its antistrophe is interposed a
     stanza outside the strophic responsion, termed a mesode,
     whose prevailing meter is ionic ($\smile\smile--$). The first strophic

grant good fortune to the house's   785
rulers, who long to see
the rule of order!
For the sake of Justice has my every word been uttered;
Zeus, be her protector!

MESODE 1

Ah! Set him before his foes
that are inside the palace,   790
Zeus, for if you exalt him to greatness,
twofold and threefold shall be
your reward at your pleasure!

ANTISTROPHE 1

And know that the orphaned colt of a sire dear to you
is harnessed in the chariot   795
of calamity; do you regulate
his running, and give it
the rhythm of those that come home safely,
so that over this course we see straining forward
a gallop that reaches the goal!

STROPHE 2

And do you who within the house inhabit   800
the inner chamber whose wealth gives joy,
give ear, gods that feel with us!
Come! . . .
redeem the blood of deeds done long ago
by a new act of justice!   805

---

pair with mesode (783–99) contains a final prayer for success to Zeus; the second (800–19) contains successive prayers
to the household gods of Agamemnon's palace, to Apollo,
and to Hermes; the third (820–37) exhorts ORESTES to carry
out with resolution the awful duty that awaits him.

791   Again the prayer appeals to the deity's self-interest; compare
255f with note.

800   This prayer is addressed to such household deities as Zeus
Ktesios, god of the storeroom (see *Agam.* 1038 with note);
Hestia, goddess of the hearth (see *Agam.* 1056 with note),
etc.

May ancient murder no longer bear its offspring in the house!

MESODE 2

And do you who dwell in the mighty cavern, fair built,
grant that our hero's house may in prosperity look up once
    more,
and that the light of freedom
may look on him with friendly   810
eyes, out of her veil!

ANTISTROPHE 2

And may Maia's son in all justice give him help,
for he has greatest power
to waft, if he will, the action to success;
and much that lies in darkness he shall illumine, if he will.   815
I utter a mysterious word:
by night he sets darkness before men's eyes,
and by day he is no plainer to the view.

STROPHE 3

And then at last, glorious,
bringing release from fear,   820
shrill, showing that the breeze is fair,
sung high by charmers of the winds,
shall the song be on our lips: "Our ship goes well!"

---

806   For the notion that one murder may beget another, compare *Agam.* 753; above 648; etc.

807   The god addressed is Apollo, Lord of Delphi. Before Apollo's coming, the oracle had belonged to the earthgoddess; the ancients believed that beneath the temple there was a chasm through which the divine influence came up from the earth to be communicated to the prophetess (see Dodds, *The Greeks and the Irrational*, Chap. III).

812   *Maia:* pronounce *My´·a.*
      Once again Hermes is prayed to; see note on 727 above.

818   Hermes can make himself invisible night or day by virtue of the "cap of Hades," the Greek equivalent of the Tarnhelm stolen by Wotan and Loge from Alberich.

For me, for me profit is now augmented, and destruction   825
stands far from those I love.

MESODE 3

And do you with courage, when there comes
the time for you to act, when she cries
to you, "My child!" utter your father's name,
your father's, and accomplish   830
an act of horror none can blame!

ANTISTROPHE 3

Maintain in your breast
the heart of a Perseus
and for your dear ones below the earth
and above, assume instead of love
a grim temper, and inside the house   835
work bloody ruin, and destroy
him who is guilty of murder.

Enter AEGISTHUS.

AEGISTHUS   I have come not unsummoned, but at a
    messenger's request;
and I hear that certain strangers have come
bringing news in no way welcome,   840
news of Orestes' death. This too will be for the house
a blood-dripping burden, still festering
and galled as it is by the bloodshed before.
How am I to suppose this tale is true and real?

---

832   *Perseus:* pronounce *Pers'·yuse:* Perseus was sent to kill the
    Gorgon Medusa, whose face none could see without being
    turned to stone; Athene therefore lent him her shield, so that
    he could see the Gorgon's reflection on its surface as he
    aimed his stroke.

840   Even AEGISTHUS as a kinsman pretends to feel sorrow at
    the news of ORESTES' death. His extreme eagerness to ques-
    tion the messenger in person, however, betrays his hope that
    the news may prove true, besides having the unfortunate
    consequence of causing him to hurry into the trap.

Is this a story born of women's terror   845
that darts upward and perishes in vain?
What can you tell me of these things that will make the
    matter clear to my mind?

    CHORUS We have heard the story, but question the
      strangers
when you have gone inside! What messengers can do is
    nothing
compared with questions put by man to man.   850

    AEGISTHUS I wish to see the messenger and to
      question him with care;
was he himself nearby when Orestes died,
or did he learn from vague report what he has told us?
He can by no means deceive a mind whose eyes are open.

    Exit AEGISTHUS.

    CHORUS *Zeus, Zeus, what can I say, where can I begin*   855
my prayer and invocation of the gods?
In my loyalty
how can I find words to match the need?
For now blood shall stain
the edges of the blades that slaughter men;   860
these will either bring disaster complete
on Agamemnon's house,
or else, kindling a torch to win freedom
and power to rule the city
Orestes shall possess the great wealth of his fathers.   865
Such is the bout which as sole antagonist of two
godlike Orestes is about to join;
and may it lead to triumph!

---

845 The metaphor is from sparks flying upward from a bonfire.

854 The metaphor of the "mind's eye" is not uncommon in
     Greek poetry.

855 The interval between the exit of AEGISTHUS and his death
     is filled in by a short choral passage of marching anapaests
     (compare note on 719). This time the only god invoked is
     Zeus.

The death-cry of AEGISTHUS is heard from inside.

CHORUS *Aha!*   870
How do things stand? How is the issue determined for the
*   house?*

Let us stand aside while the affair is being settled,
that we may seem guiltless in this trouble;
for now has the issue of the battle been decided.

Enter SLAVE.

SLAVE Woe! Utter woe! The master is struck down!   875
Woe yet again for the third time I cry!
Aegisthus is no more! Come, open up
as quickly as you can, unbar the doors
of the women's rooms! We need a right strong arm—
not to help him who is already dead; what need?   880

He shouts.

My shout falls on deaf ears; to folk that lie in ineffective
    sleep
I utter futile words. Where is Clytemnestra? What is she at?
Now, it seems, near her consort
shall her head in turn fall, smitten by the stroke of justice.

Enter CLYTEMNESTRA.

CLYTEMNESTRA What is the matter? Why do you raise
the alarm in the house?   885

---

870 These lines are in lyric iambics, the lyric meter closest to
     the iambics of dialogue and therefore usually chosen for
     isolated lyric utterances similar to ordinary dialogue.

879 The strong man is needed to open the doors at once, as a
     parallel passage in the *Odyssey* (23. 187) helps to show;
     with grim irony the SLAVE goes on to make it clear that he
     is not calling for a strong man in order to save AEGISTHUS.

883 This line contains a textual crux; the translation adopts a
     possible emendation.

SLAVE   A living man, I say, is slain by the dead. //

CLYTEMNESTRA   Ah woe! I understand your words, despite the riddle!
By guile shall we perish, just as we slew by guile!
In all speed give me a man-slaying axe!
Let us know if we are the victors or the vanquished;   890
yes, so far along the path of catastrophe have I come!

> ORESTES and PYLADES become visible, and near them the body of AEGISTHUS.

ORESTES   You are the one I seek; this man has had enough.

CLYTEMNESTRA   Oh woe! You are dead, dearest one, mighty Aegisthus!

ORESTES   Do you hold the man dear? Then in the same tomb
you shall lie, and in death shall you never lose him.   895

---

886   This alludes to the false report of ORESTES' death.

889   Several vase paintings not far removed in date from the *Oresteia* show CLYTEMNESTRA using an axe in this scene; an axe might be at hand even in a house expecting no attack. This may be the origin of the story used by Sophocles in his *Electra* and by Euripides in several plays that Agamemnon was killed with an axe. In Aeschylus there is a notable imprecision about the weapon Agamemnon was killed with, perhaps because Aeschylus wanted to focus on the fatal garment that was thrown over him; perhaps it was a sword (see note on *Agam.* page 91). ORESTES and PYLADES, together with the body, came into view probably by means of the device known as the *ekkyklema*, a kind of platform which could be wheeled or pushed forward to disclose the scene behind the stage door. (Compare note on *Agam.* 1372f.)

CLYTEMNESTRA Hold, my son, and have respect, my
    child,
for this breast, at which many a time in slumber
have you sucked with your gums the milk that nourished
    you!

ORESTES Pylades, what am I to do? Shall I respect my
    mother, and not kill her?

PYLADES Where henceforth shall be the oracles of
    Loxias   900
declared at Pytho, and the covenant you pledged on oath?
Count all man your enemies rather than the gods!

ORESTES I judge you the victor, and your advice is
    good.

    To CLYTEMNESTRA.

Come this way! I wish to kill you by his very side!
For in life you preferred him to my father.   905
Sleep by his side in death, since you love
this man, while him you should have loved you hate!

---

896 The word translated "respect" here and at 899 is *aidos*, which
     basically means the respect or consideration one owes to
     any person because of his status; it is often used of those
     who give in to the entreaties of a suppliant, and hence in
     some contexts it is not far from meaning "pity." It is espe-
     cially applicable to the respect owed to parents. According to
     a well-known story, Helen, when recaptured by Menelaus
     during the sack of Troy, moved him to spare her life by
     showing him her bare breast.

900 These are the only words spoken by PYLADES. As the son of
     the king of Phocis and a neighbor of the Delphic god, he
     is well qualified to be his spokesman here; his name suggests
     Pylai, the meeting place of the Amphictyonic League, which
     protected Delphi.

901 *Pytho:* pronounce *Pie'·tho.*

CLYTEMNESTRA It was I who reared you, and I would
grow old with you.

ORESTES What! Shall you, my father's killer, share my
home?

CLYTEMNESTRA Fate, my son, must share the blame for
this.   910

ORESTES Then this your doom also has been sent by
Fate.

CLYTEMNESTRA Have you no awe of a parent's curse, my
son?

ORESTES No, for you gave me birth and yet cast me out
into misfortune.

CLYTEMNESTRA I did not cast you out when I sent you
to the house of an ally.

ORESTES Vilely was I sold, though born of a free father. 915

CLYTEMNESTRA Then where is the price I got for you?

ORESTES I am ashamed to taunt you outright with that.

CLYTEMNESTRA Name also the follies of your father!

ORESTES Do not reproach him who labored, you who
sat at home!

CLYTEMNESTRA It is a cruel thing for wives to be separated from a husband, my son.   920

---

908 These lines are in the standard form of dialogue called
stichomythia; see note on 108.

915 For the notion that ORESTES has been sold by his mother,
compare 132f; the price was of course her relationship with
AEGISTHUS.

918 The reference is to Chryseis (see the first book of *The Iliad*),
Cassandra, and others.

ORESTES Yes, but the husband's toil supports them while they sit inside.

CLYTEMNESTRA It seems, my child, that you will kill your mother.

ORESTES You yourself, I say, not I will be your slayer.

CLYTEMNESTRA Take care, beware your mother's wrathful hounds!

EITHER WAY HE'S A LOSER.

ORESTES And how shall I escape my father's, if I neglect this duty?   925

CLYTEMNESTRA I am like one who, still alive, laments to her own grave in vain.

ORESTES Yes, for it is my father's fate sends you this doom.

CLYTEMNESTRA Ah woe, that I bore and reared this serpent!

ORESTES In truth the fear your dream inspired was prophetic!

---

921 Hesiod in the *Theogony* (398f) had compared women with drones, who sit in the hive and live off the production of the working bees. ORESTES' language in this passage echoes much misogynistic matter in early Greek poetry.

924 The Erinyes are often called "hounds," and in *The Eumenides* they are depicted as picking up a scent and pursuing their quarry just as hounds do (see *Eum.* 131f, 246f).

925 It must be remembered that if ORESTES had not killed his mother, the Erinyes would have pursued him for failing to avenge his father; in that event he would not have had the protection of Apollo; compare 276f.

926 CLYTEMNESTRA calls ORESTES "a tomb" because of his insensibility; there was a proverb that "pleading with a stupid man is like pleading with a tomb." But ORESTES makes her words apply not to himself but to his father.

928 CLYTEMNESTRA remembers her warning dream (see 526f).

Wrong was the murder that you did, wrong is the fate that
    now you suffer! 930

    Exit ORESTES dragging CLYTEMNESTRA's body
    with him.

CHORUS Even for these I lament in their twofold disaster;
yet since sorely tried Orestes has mounted to the peak
of many deeds of blood, we choose rather to have it thus,
so that the eye of the house may not be utterly extinguished.

STROPHE 1

There came Justice in time to the sons of Priam, 935
there came a heavy retribution;
and there has come to the house of Agamemnon
twice a lion, twice a god of war!
Altogether he has got his inheritance,
he, the exile prompted by Pytho, 940
well sped on his course by the counsels of the gods!

MESODE

Cry out in triumph at the escape of our master's palace

---

930 In accordance with the normal rules of Attic drama, the
killing probably took place off stage.

934 The eye was accounted the most precious part of the body,
and the most precious part of anything might therefore be
referred to as its "eye."

935 The CHORUS sings an ode of triumph, entirely in the
dochmiac meter. For the basic rhythm of dochmiacs, see the
note on 152-63; they are regularly used to express agitation
or excitement. As in the Second Stasimon, a mesode stands
between each strophe and its antistrophe (942-45, 962-64).

935 Once again, as so often in *Agamemnon*, a parallel is drawn
between the just punishment of the house of Priam and the
just punishment of the house of Atreus; only here CLYTEM-
NESTRA and AEGISTHUS are in question.

938 ORESTES and PYLADES are probably referred to.

from evil and the wasting of its substance
beneath the rule of two polluters,
a grievous fortune!   945

ANTISTROPHE 1

And there has come one who directs war by stealth,
the crafty Hermes;
and there guided his hand in the battle the trueborn
daughter of Zeus—Justice is the name
we mortals give her, hitting the mark—   950
breathing upon her foes her deadly wrath.

STROPHE 2

Even this did Loxias, he who occupies
the mighty cavern of the land of Parnassus,
loudly proclaim; with guileless guile   955
does he visit mischief grown inveterate;
and ever somehow does the divine prevail,
so that we do not serve the wicked;
it is right to reverence the power that has the mastery of
   heaven.   960

---

946 In this stanza—if the text I have adopted is right—Hermes, Zeus, and Zeus together with his daughter Justice are praised for their part in the revenge; Apollo is praised in the following stanza (953f). Zeus, Apollo, and Hermes are all prayed to in the two opening strophic pairs of the Second Stasimon (783f with notes).

948 The name of Justice—in Attic Greek *Dike*, but in the dialect of choral lyric *Dika*—is here derived from *Dios kora*, "daughter of Zeus." In terms of modern scientific etymology the derivation is absurd; but in early Greece belief in the magical significance of names was widespread (compare, e.g., *Agam.* 681f), and many etymologies that cannot possibly be valid were taken seriously. In his dialogue *Cratylus*, Plato discusses many etymologies of this kind; just how seriously he took them is not easy to determine.

953 See 807f above. Parnassus is the mountain on whose slopes the Delphic temple stands; for the name "Loxias," see note on 558.

MESODE

Now can we see the light, and the great curb
has been lifted from the household.
Arise, O house! For all too long
have you lain prostrate.

ANTISTROPHE 2

And soon shall all-accomplishing time pass   965
the portals of the palace, when from its hearth
all pollution shall be driven
by means of a cleansing which expels destruction.
In the light of a fortune fair to look on can we see
the whole, as we cry out,   970
"The tenants of the house shall be cast out."
Now we can see the light!

> A crowd of Argive citizens, admitted to the palace
> by order of ORESTES to hear his speech, enters
> the stage, and the fatal garment used in the
> murder of AGAMEMNON is displayed near the dead
> bodies of CLYTEMNESTRA and AEGISTHUS.

ORESTES   Look upon the two tyrants of the land,
the spoilers of my house who killed my father!
Majestic were they then, seated upon their thrones,   975
and dear to each other even now, as we may read by the fate

---

965   To us this personification of time seems strangely artificial,
but in Greek it is not uncommon; compare those examples at
Agam. 894, 985.

971   The "tenants of the house" are the Erinyes, who have so long
beset it; compare *Agam.* 1186f.

973   In this scene the bodies remain visible, and the fatal garment
in which Agamemnon was entangled is displayed. It is a
reasonable surmise that the stage is occupied not only by
the CHORUS but by others representing the people of Argos
summoned to the palace by ORESTES. Each of ORESTES'
opening speeches (973–1006, 1010–17) is followed by a brief
utterance by the CHORUS in marching anapests, the two
anapestic passages being exactly symmetrical.

they have suffered; and their covenant abides by its sworn
    terms.
Together they swore death for my unhappy father,
and together they swore to die; and they have kept their oath.

Look also, you who take cognizance of this sad work,   980
on the device they used, to bind my unhappy father,
their manacles for his hands and fetters for his feet!
Spread it out! Stand by in a circle,
and display her covering for her husband, that the father
    may behold
—not my father, but he who looks upon this whole world,   985
the Sun!—may behold my mother's unholy work,
so that he may bear me witness on the day of judgment
    when it comes
that it was with justice that I pursued this killing—

---

977 i.e., "they abide by the sworn terms of their covenant."

978 (See note on 434.) ORESTES imagines his mother and her
     lover as having said, "May we die, if only we can kill Aga-
     memnon!" Since they did indeed conspire together to kill
     him, and a conspiracy according to ancient ways of thought
     involves an oath, he can speak of them as having *sworn* to
     kill Agamemnon and to die together, and as having kept
     their oath.

980 The word translated "take cognizance" has legal connota-
     tions; ORESTES is formally calling his audience to witness the
     guilt of the people he has put to death, displaying as his
     evidence the instrument of murder.

985 From Homer's time onwards it was common to call upon
     the all-seeing Sun to witness actions that had taken place
     within its view.

987 What possible occasion does ORESTES have in mind? He is
     aware that he may have to give an account of his action;
     later he has to justify it before the Areopagus with the
     Erinyes as his prosecutors.

that of my mother (for Aegisthus' death I count for nothing;
he has suffered the adulterer's penalty, as is the law).   990
What name am I to give this thing, speak I never so fair?   997
A trap for a wild beast, or, draped over the dead man's feet,
the draping of a coffin? No, a net,
a hunting-net, you might call it, or a robe to entangle a man's
    feet.   1000
Such a possession might some brigand set,
a cheater of travelers who plays a robber's trade,
and with this cunning snare
might he slay many a man and much delight his heart
    thereby.   1004
But she who devised this hateful deed against her hus-
    band,   991
whose children she had borne beneath her girdle,
a burden once dear, but now of deadly hatred, as the sight
    of her reveals,
what think you of her? Had she been a sea-snake or a viper,
would not her very touch have had power to rot another
    yet unbitten,   995
such was her shamelessness and evil pride!

---

989   According to fifth-century Athenian law, a man might law-
fully put to death the seducer of his wife; the first speech
of the orator Lysias is a defense of a man who had done
so.

997   The transposition adopted in the text was suggested only
during the present century, but it removes more than one
serious difficulty better than other suggested expedients.

998   The word used for "coffin" originally meant "bath," and
the phrase is obviously meant to suggest the bath in which
Agamemnon was murdered. The words, indeed, mean "the
curtain of a bath," and they are thus a doubly apt description
of the object in question.

1001   ORESTES imagines that an object like the robe might be a
suitable device for some atrocious brigand like Procrustes,
Sciron, or the other criminals punished by Theseus.

May I never have such a mate to share   1005
my house! Sooner than that, may the gods make me perish
    childless!

    CHORUS Alas, alas, for woeful work!
Hateful the death by which you were undone!
Alas, alas!
And for him that survives suffering now ripens to the full.

    ORESTES *Confidence losing* Did she do the deed or not? This robe   1010
is my witness, as to how Aegisthus' sword dyed it.
And the blood that gushed forth was time's partner
in spoiling the many dyes applied to the embroidery.
Now do I speak his eulogy, now am I here to render him
    due lamentation;
and as I call upon this web that slew my father   1015
I grieve for what was done and what was suffered and for all
    our race,
bearing as I do the unenviable pollution of this victory.

1005 Childlessness for an ancient Greek was one of the worst
possible disasters, so that the final words are more emphatic
than they might seem.

1007 These are marching anapests; see note at the beginning of
the scene.

1010 Again ORESTES uses legal language.

1011 This does not necessarily imply that CLYTEMNESTRA bor-
rowed a sword from AEGISTHUS with which to murder
Agamemnon. We know that the body was mutilated after
death, and it was a common practice in the ancient world
to stab again and again the dead body of a hated enemy,
as the Greeks did that of Hector (*Iliad* 22. 371).

1014 CLYTEMNESTRA had outraged her dead husband by de-
priving him of the rite of lamentation by his nearest kin
(*Agam.* 1548–59 with notes); now ORESTES is here to
discharge the duty that he could not perform then.

1017 For the Greeks the essence of victory was that it should

CHORUS *None among mortals shall pass his whole life*
    free from suffering,
enjoying honor to the end.
Alas, alas!
One sorrow comes today, another shall come tomorrow.   1020

ORESTES But I would have you know—for I do not know
    how it will end—
I am like a man in a chariot driving my team
far from the course; for my wits are hard to govern
and carry me away, losing the battle; and close to my heart
fear is ready to sing, and my heart to dance in anger to its
    tune.   1025
And while I am still sane, I make proclamation to my
    friends,
and I declare that not without justice did I slay my mother,
the polluted murderess of my father and an object loathed
    of heaven.
And among the promptings that urged me to the deed, I
    give first place
to the prophet of Pytho, Loxias, whose oracle told me   1030
that if I did this thing I should be free
of guilt, but if I did not—I will not name the penalty;
for no man's arrow shall reach that height of woe.

---

be enviable, so that the expression used here is a kind of
bitter paradox. An untranslatable particle in 1016 indicates that although ORESTES laments for all that has happened, he would not change what he has just done.

1018   These are again marching anapests, symmetrical with those
       at 1007-9; for the commonplace that they express, com-
       pare *Agam.* 1341-42.

1021   The metaphor of "going off the course" is used to describe
       the onset of madness, not only here, but in *Prometheus*
       when Io goes mad (883-84).

1033   The sense appears to be that if all the troubles were piled

And now behold me, and see how, armed
with this branch and wreath, I shall approach as sup-
    pliant   1035
the dwelling at earth's navel, the domain of Loxias,
and the light of the fire called everlasting,
an exile for the shedding of this kindred blood; for to no
    other hearth
did Loxias order me to turn.
This command I lay upon all men of Argos, as time goes
    on   1040
to remember how the evil was brought about,
and to bear me witness, when Menelaus shall come.
But I, a wanderer, an exile from this land,
in life and death leaving this report of me . . .

             . . . . . .

CHORUS Why, your act was noble! Let not evil
    slander
gag your mouth, do not speak any ill-omened words!   1045

---

           on one another you could not shoot an arrow high enough
           to reach the top.

1035   Suppliants approaching the altar of a god carried boughs
           and wore garlands.

1036   Delphi was believed to be at the center of the earth.

1037   Many Greek altars had fires burning on them which were
           supposed never to go out. If they were put out (as happened,
           for example, when the temples of Athens were destroyed in
           480 B.C. by the Persians under Xerxes), they had to be
           renewed from Delphi.

1041   *Menelaus:* pronounce *Men·e·lay′·us.*

           In the manuscript two lines have been made into one by
           mistake; the text has been conjecturally restored. The
           satyr-play that accompanied the *Oresteia, Proteus,* re-
           counted the adventures of Menelaus after he had been
           separated from Agamemnon's ship by the storm described
           at *Agam.* 636f.

You have liberated the whole state of Argos,
lopping the heads of two serpents with dexterous stroke.

ORESTES Ah, ah! *comf* ↓ *AH yes* *CHORUS SAYS THE WORD.*
Here are ghastly women, like Gorgons,
with dark raiment and thick-clustered snakes
for tresses! I cannot stay!   **1050**
        ↓ *THE FURIES- CHTHONIC VENGEFUL & PURSUING*

CHORUS What are these fancies, O truest of all men to
    your father,
that vex you? Stay, do not be afraid for your victory is great!

ORESTES Fancies have no part in these troubles for me;
for I know that these are my mother's wrathful hounds.

CHORUS Yes, for the blood is still fresh upon your
    hands.   **1055**
It is that makes turmoil come upon your mind.

ORESTES O lord Apollo, see, they multiply;
and they drip from their eyes a hateful stream.

CHORUS There is but one way of cleansing; Loxias by
    his touch
will free you from these troubles.   **1060**

ORESTES You do not see these, but I see them!
They hound me on, I cannot stay!

CHORUS Good luck go with you, and may the god
    watch over you
and guard you in his kindness, so that your fortune prospers!

    Exit ORESTES.

Now upon the royal house   **1065**

1048 Only ORESTES can see the Erinyes; but in the last play of
    the trilogy, *The Eumenides,* they are visible to everyone be-
    cause they form the Chorus.

1054 See note on 924 above.

1065 The CHORUS finishes with marching anapests, listing the

for yet a third time has the tempest
blown and proved grievous!
First came the eating of children's flesh,
the cruel woes of Thyestes;
Then were the sorrows of the king, the husband,   1070
when slaughtered in his bath there fell
the war lord of the Achaeans;
and now thirdly has there come from somewhere a
    deliverer—
or shall I say a doom?
What shall be the decision, what the end   1075
of the might of destruction, lulled at last to rest?

---

      three successive visitations of the curse upon the family and
      inquiring what is to be the family's future.

1069   *Thyestes:* pronounce *Thi·ess'·tēs.*

1072   *Achaeans:* pronounce A·*kee'·ans.*

1073   There is an allusion to "Zeus the Preserver who comes
       third," a title that derives from the pouring of the third
       libation at a banquet in honor of Zeus the Preserver (cf.
       Agam. 245f, 1385–86).

1076   The play ends with the ominous word *ate,* "destruction."

BIBLIOGRAPHY

No adequate commentary on *The Libation Bearers* exists in English; A. Sidgwick's school edition (*Aeschylus, Choephori*: London: Oxford University Press, 2nd ed., 1902) is useful.